IT'S RIGGED IN YOUR

FAVOR

DESTINY IMAGE BOOKS BY KEVIN L. ZADAI

Supernatural Finances

The Agenda of Angels

Praying from the Heavenly Realms

IT'S RIGGED IN YOUR
FAVOR

HOW WOULD YOU LIVE IF
YOU KNEW YOU WOULDN'T FAIL?

KEVIN L. ZADAI

DEDICATION

I dedicate this book to the Lord Jesus Christ. When I died during surgery and met with Jesus on the other side, He insisted that I return to life on the earth and that I help people with their destinies. Because of Jesus's love and concern for people, the Lord has actually chosen to send a person back from death to help everyone who will receive that help so that his or her destiny and purpose is secure in Him. I want You, Lord, to know that when You come to take me to be with You someday, it is my sincere hope that people remember not me, but the revelation of Jesus Christ that You have revealed through me. I want others to know that I am merely being obedient to Your heavenly calling and mission, which is to reveal Your plan for the fulfillment of the divine destiny for each of God's children.

ACKNOWLEDGMENTS

In addition to sharing my story with everyone through the books *Heavenly Visitation: A Guide to the Supernatural, Days of Heaven on Earth: A Guide to the Days Ahead, A Meeting Place with God, Your Hidden Destiny Revealed, Praying from the Heavenly Realms: Supernatural Secrets to a Lifestyle of Answered Prayer,* and *The Agenda of Angels: What the Holy Ones Want You to Know About the Next Move of God* the Lord gave me a commission to produce this book, *It's Rigged in Your Favor.* This book addresses some of the revelations concerning the areas that Jesus reviewed and revealed to me through the Word of God and by the Spirit of God during several visitations. I want to thank everyone who has encouraged me, assisted me and prayed for me during the writing of this work, especially my spiritual parents, Dr. Jesse Duplantis and Dr. Cathy Duplantis. Special thanks to my wonderful wife Kathi for her love and dedication to the Lord and to me. Thank you, Sid Roth and staff, for your love of our supernatural Messiah, Jesus. Thank you, Dr. Janet Kline, for the wonderful job editing this book. Thank you, Destiny Image and staff, for your support of this project. Special thanks, as well, to all my friends who know about how *it's all rigged in our favor* and how Jesus would want us to live as though we could not lose in the next move of God's Spirit!

CONTENTS

Foreword *by Dr. Keith Ellis* 1

Foreword *by Sid Roth*.........................3

Introduction.................................7

CHAPTER 1   When Favor Takes Over...................... 11

CHAPTER 2   Your Personal Book of Destiny................. 29

CHAPTER 3   The Lord Knows You Personally............... 39

CHAPTER 4   God Plans Your Journey 59

CHAPTER 5   The Father's Hand Brings Impartation.......... 79

CHAPTER 6   His Spirit Guides You 95

CHAPTER 7   The I AM Is with You....................... 109

CHAPTER 8   The Lord Created You....................... 123

CHAPTER 9   The Lord Has Written About You............. 139

CHAPTER 10   The Lord Thinks About You 153

CHAPTER 11   The Lord Protects You as a Mighty Warrior.... 167

CHAPTER 12   The Lord Searches Your Heart 193

CHAPTER 13   The Foreknowledge of the Almighty........... 207

CHAPTER 14   You Are Chosen 223

CHAPTER 15   You Can Outlast the Devil 237

Salvation Prayer............................ 257

FOREWORD

DR. KEVIN ZADAI HAS DONE IT AGAIN—HIS LATEST work is a powerful exhortation to the Body of Christ that will, no doubt, mark a historical turning point and a new season of revival for the modern church. Furthermore, I believe this book is an outstanding resource for restoration and healing for all who seek a fresh anointing of the Holy Spirit. I am continually amazed at how God uses Dr. Kevin Zadai to write about the heart of the Father in ways that few have experienced. Dr. Zadai's revelatory encounter of being caught up into the glory of Heaven should give every believer encouragement, hope, and an expectation of wonderful things to come. Following his supernatural experience, Dr. Zadai has repeatedly, and without fail, delivered revelation knowledge like fresh manna to all who hunger for the next mighty move of God, and I cannot get enough.

I believe that this particular book, with its extraordinary title, is an invitation to experience the depths of abundance that Jesus has prepared for us, both in this life and for all eternity. Dr. Kevin Zadai and his wife Kathi have become some of the dearest friends I have ever had, with a true heart for the hurting. With each new book, teaching, and sermon they deliver, I am uplifted, encouraged, and strengthened through revelation upon revelation. I am so honored to have this opportunity to write the foreword to this book, as I believe it is a work to bring the Body of Christ to the next level and prepare us all for a sweeping move of God's glory upon the earth. While reading this book, you better buckle up, because you're about to experience heights you've never encountered before. If you're waiting and ready for the next level, this is it! Thank you, Kevin, for this mighty word from God and thank You, Jesus!

Dr. Keith Ellis

FOREWORD

I HAVE INTERVIEWED DR. KEVIN ZADAI MANY TIMES on my television show, *It's Supernatural!,* and he has become a good friend. What makes Kevin unique is the Glory, or manifest Presence of God, that accompanies him. This heavenly atmosphere has surrounded him since he died, went to heaven, and returned. Not only does Kevin carry this heavenly Glory, but when he was in heaven God downloaded to him a lifetime of revelation. Each new book he writes contains a portion of this revelation.

God instructed Kevin to tell all believers this most encouraging word: *"You can't fail because it is all rigged in your favor!"* But this word is **only** true for His **obedient** children. If you have failed many times and feel like you are in a hopeless situation right now, I have good news. The true meaning of "grace" is God's enabling power to overcome sin.

I live in instant repentance. The moment I catch myself in a sinful thought or action, I repent. This prevents the thought or action from becoming a demonic stronghold. The only fear I have is that I don't want to disappoint God. I believe this is what the Bible means when it speaks of the fear of the Lord. I practice a lifestyle of what God told the early believers in First John 1:9: *"**If** we confess our sins, He is faithful and just to forgive us our sins and cleanse us from **all** unrighteousness."*

What did God mean when he told Kevin, *"It is all rigged in your favor"*? He was referring to the Book of Life. During the Days of Awe (the ten days between the Feast of Trumpets and the Day of Atonement), we Jews say to one another, "May your name be inscribed in The Book of Life." This book is described in Daniel 12:1: *"...your people shall be delivered, every one who is found written in the **book**."*

I have interviewed many believers like Kevin who have seen these books in heaven. These books not only record when we will die, but everything we are created to do in our life. It is all good. That's why God wants you to know, *"You can't fail because it is all rigged in your favor!"* But we are all given a free will and the devil will take advantage of our ignorance on how to operate in faith in the Word of God instead of our flesh.

This is why God gave us our own angel, the Bible, the gift of tongues, and the Holy Spirit. I am convinced that when we pray in tongues, we are praying out our destiny in the Book of Life. I am also convinced that when we read the Bible and act on what it says, we are invincible.

The same Glory that surrounds Kevin is now increasing on those believers who are hungry for more. It is like the river flowing from the Temple in Ezekiel 47. First the water level reached the ankles, then it rose high enough to swim in.

The water represents the Glory. The level of Glory we are seeing is up to our big toes now, but very soon we will be swimming in the Glory. This will be the game changer in your life and this generation. The promises of God will be instant. You will operate in every miracle Jesus did and even greater!

The devil thinks he has won in your life and destiny. But in this Greater Glory God wants you to know: *You can't fail because it is all rigged in your favor!*

SID ROTH
Host, *It's Supernatural!*

INTRODUCTION

BEING IN THE HEAVENLY REALMS WITH JESUS CHRIST is beyond anyone's ability to comprehend. When I came back to this earthly realm, it took some time and adjustment between what I knew was true from the visitation and what was happening in my environment at the present time in this earth realm. It seemed at times that there were two different worlds, and I wondered how to define the boundaries between the two and live successfully in both at the same time.

I began to use the principles that Jesus taught me by the power of the Holy Spirit, implementing them into my life with great results. It did not come quickly or easily at first, but through persistence I felt a great breakthrough and began to understand how to live in both realms simultaneously.

One day, when I was traveling and doing conferences, I was sitting in a coffee shop with a group of minister friends.

As we sat and talked and sipped our coffee, I looked behind the ministers and was astounded to see that Jesus had walked up and was standing behind them. The power of God was so strong, but they did not seem to know He was there.

Jesus looked right at me to get my attention and candidly asked me to present a question to my minister friends at the table. Jesus said, "Ask them how they would live tomorrow if they knew they could not fail." So I asked the question Jesus wanted me to relay to them. I can tell you that their mental capacity couldn't wrap around what was just said. Because of this fallen world and the way that we have been trained to believe, it is beyond our mental capacity to think that failure can be eliminated. At first thought, it seems that Jesus Himself could not even appear to us and help us out of our dilemmas.

After giving them some time to think about it, I suggested that they begin to plan their life out with this framework of thinking—*it's all rigged in your favor*. In Heaven, God has never planned for you to fail even though you may have already done so. There has never been an angel sent that thought he was going to fail, and yet failure seems to be prevalent in many Christians' lives. On the day of Pentecost, when the Holy Spirit was sent, He never once thought He was going to fail. Since your spirit was born again by the Holy Spirit on the day that you confessed Jesus as Lord, the Holy Spirit within you has never thought about failure once in your case.

The books that are written about you in Heaven must come to pass. Each one of your days was written before one of them came to pass (see Ps. 139:16). God has amazing plans for you, and the angels of the Lord of Heaven have been sent to help implement those plans so that you can glorify God in this life and live in two realms at once. So I ask you the same question. How would you live tomorrow if you knew you couldn't fail? All of Heaven is waiting for your reply. God and the cloud of witnesses all believe in you and are ready to change your course in this life so that you can become the history maker you were destined to be.

KEVIN L. ZADAI, ThD

Chapter 1

WHEN FAVOR
TAKES OVER

Lord, how wonderfully you bless the righteous.
Your favor wraps around each one and covers
them under your canopy of kindness and joy.
—PSALM 5:12 TPT

I REMEMBER THE DAY WHEN THINGS TURNED AND I began to have tremendous favor in my life. It was the day that the tables turned against my enemy and I no longer lived as a victim. This change must happen in every believer's life, and the sooner it happens the better. I can tell you where I was standing when I was touched by the Holy Spirit with revelation and saw that I was no longer a victim but that my enemy was now the victim!

It all began one morning several years ago, as I woke up. I remember sensing in my spirit that things had changed.

It was as if I knew I had the advantage over satan. I realized that my spirit had been built up by the Word of God and by praying in tongues, which had overthrown certain areas in my life. It seemed as though it literally happened overnight. I was overwhelmed with the feeling that everything now had been rigged in my favor.

As I stood by my bed, I began to address the enemy, instructing him with accuracy and confidence what he was to do and not do. It was as if I was staring my enemy down, knowing that he had to back off and was afraid of me. From that day on, I knew that I was to never back off from what I know concerning my position in Jesus Christ. As the months followed after this encounter, I started to see increased favor taking over my life. I was no longer a victim but was highly favored by God, and I knew it.

I could sense a greater authority in my words as I spoke and walked with God. It was all part of the favor of God taking over my life. It has gotten to the place where I see my prayers answered without even uttering them. It's as if God reads and hears my heart without words. I started to encounter the glory of God in my meditation and prayer times. As the glory became stronger, I even started to see physical changes in my house for the better. Every single area of my life started to increase with favor as the glory of God began to be revealed.

Evil spirits will eventually realize that they are pushing you into the glory of the Father. The evil spirits recognize that it is counterproductive for them to continue to harass a Christian who is no longer a victim in their mind. I began to treat evil spirits as victims and harass them. The Lord began to work with me, confirming His Word with signs and wonders following (see Mark 16:20). I remember thinking how so many of my friends and acquaintances needed this same type of encounter to occur in their own lives.

Does God have favorites? Well, I do know this; He has a way of making each one of His children feel as though they are His only favorite child. I remember spending time with Jesus in 1992 when He appeared to me. I recall His love for me and how He believed in me more than any other person I knew. As I looked into His eyes, I was captured by His love for me. Up until that time, I didn't know how extreme His passion is for each one us. He had bought me, and I was worth the price! By the time He was done revealing His plans for me and explaining how much He believed in me, I was convinced that I was His favorite! He has this way of making all His children who love and obey Him experience this. I had become irresistible to Him before I was even born, and He had written about me in a book. This revelation overwhelmed me, and I came back to this earth fully convinced that I was His favorite and could not fail. My assignment now is to convince others that it is the same in their life as well.

Our loving heavenly Father reveals ways for us to increase in the area of favor in our life. There are some things that we can do to encounter *overwhelming favor*. But first, I want to lay a foundation through a couple of word studies concerning what the Lord showed me about *it's all rigged in your favor!*

WHAT IS FAVOR?

Favor is mentioned many times in the Word of God. In the King James Version of the Bible, the word *favour* appears 70 times. We can see that when God decides to pay attention to a specific individual or people group favorably, there are several events that occur with characteristics that include honor, success, prosperity, forgiveness, and close friendship with special privileges and benefits. To have favor with God means that you have become a friend. This is not just positional, but it is the relational side of salvation through Jesus Christ. There is a difference between what Jesus has done for us positionally (through His redemptive actions as a man who became a sacrifice) and relationally, which is our response to the work of God through Jesus and how we walk out that reality on the earth as *history makers*.

Webster's 1828 Dictionary defines *favor* as:

> To regard with kindness; to support; to aid or have the disposition to aid, or to wish success to; to be propitious to; to countenance; to befriend; to encourage. To favor the cause of a party, may be merely to wish success to it, or it may signify to give it aid, by counsel, or by active exertions.

To truly have favor with someone is when it gets to the point where their kindness goes beyond just wishing for success. It is the action of befriending you and giving you counsel and taking up your case. When you have won over the favor of God, you cannot ever pay Him back. He will make sure that everything goes according to His will for you, and you will be overcome with His goodness.

When a friend "wishes you well," you consider them to be a kind person. But a friend who wishes you wellness and success *and* has the ability to do something about it is beyond your ability to comprehend.

In *Strong's Dictionary*, *favor* (H7521) is defined as follows:

> רָצָה râṣâ; a primitive root; to be pleased with; specifically, to satisfy a debt:—(be) accept(-able), accomplish,

set affection, approve, consent with, delight (self), enjoy, (be, have a) favour(-able), like, observe, pardon, (be, have, take) please(-ure), reconcile self.

1. to be pleased with
2. be favourable to
3. accept favourably

(Qal) to be pleased with, be favourable to, to accept, to be pleased, be determined, to make acceptable, satisfy, to please
(Niphal) to be accepted, be pleased with
(Piel) to seek favour of
(Hiphil) to please, pay off
(Hithpael) to make oneself acceptable or pleasing

The idea behind the Strong's definitions is the concept of debt forgiveness and pardon. So, to win God's favor is to be completely overcome with goodness because you have gained the heart of God. Favor is not earned; we must learn to receive it. God can favor us to the point where we are acceptable and pleasing to Him. The Lord Himself pardons us and pays our debts so that we can live in freedom.

Next, I want to discuss the word *rigged*. I remember when the Lord gave me this phrase concerning *favor*. He said, "It's all *rigged* in your favor, Kevin!" Here is the definition of rigged from the Urban Dictionary:

The word rigged is used to describe situations where unfair advantages are given to one side of a conflict.

Describes the side of the conflict that holds an unfair advantage.

To have things in your favor, everything is going great, to say something of reference is cool and or awesome, an exclamation of excitement or enthusiasm.

This is exciting news to the child of God—the Lord has given you an unfair advantage! This life has been rigged in your favor. Your heavenly Father has announced that you are adopted into the family of God (see Rom. 8:15).

After receiving this phrase from the Lord, I began to see how God's children have such potential to gain favor if we agree to walk in obedience according to His Word and His Spirit. This requires a heartfelt trust known as *faith*. The writer of the book of Hebrews discusses this at length. Remember, we have a choice to believe and enter into God's favor. We can grieve our heavenly Father through doubt, unbelief, and disobedience:

> *They grieved God for forty years by sinning in their **unbelief**, until they dropped dead in the desert. So God swore an oath that they would never enter into his calming place of rest all because they **disobeyed** him. It is clear that they could not enter into their inheritance because they wrapped their hearts in **unbelief**.*
>
> *Now God has offered to us the same promise of entering into his realm of resting in confident faith. So we must be extremely careful to ensure that we all embrace the fullness of that promise and not fail to experience it. For we have heard the good news of deliverance just as they did, yet they didn't join their faith with the Word. Instead, what they heard didn't affect them deeply, for they **doubted**. For those of us who believe, faith activates the promise and we experience the realm of confident rest!*

For he has said, "I was grieved with them and made a solemn oath, 'They will never enter into the calming rest of my Spirit'" (Hebrews 3:17–4:3 TPT).

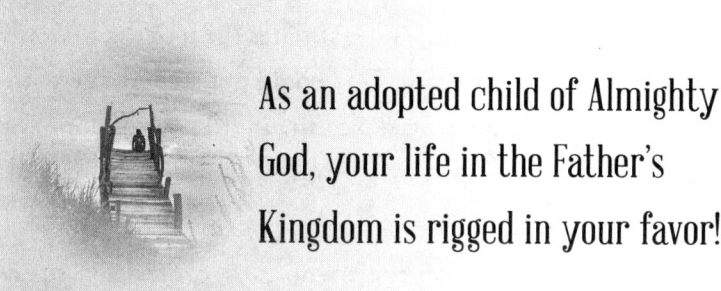

As an adopted child of Almighty God, your life in the Father's Kingdom is rigged in your favor!

God loves to observe certain character traits in His children. The book of Hebrews talks about one particular trait that we can exhibit that will please God if we develop it. The character trait is our *faith* and *diligence* in seeking Him, and that gets His attention.

Faith lifted Enoch from this life and he was taken up into heaven! He never had to experience death; he just disappeared from this world because God promoted him. For before he was translated to the heavenly realm his life had become a pleasure to God. And without faith living within us it would be impossible to please God. For we come to God in faith knowing that he is real and that he rewards the faith of those who give all their passion and strength into seeking him (Hebrews 11:5-6 TPT).

Think about Enoch and his circumstances. He did not have the same covenant that we have today through Jesus Christ. He did, however, develop an intimate relationship with God that caused extreme favor to come into his life. His faith caused the God of the universe to take notice of him. Enoch obtained favor because he pleased God.

The idea here is to passionately pursue God, knowing that He rewards those who seek Him out diligently with all the spiritual strength that they can exert. You know God is pleased when He takes someone from this earthly realm and translates them to the heavenly realm without experiencing death. God could not stand to be without Enoch because God experienced pleasure in the relationship. The faith that Enoch had developed by trusting God became irresistible to Heaven!

Today, God has redeemed people who have confessed Jesus as their Savior. Out of those redeemed people, God favors those who have implemented the promises by faith and become partakers of the divine nature.

> Grace and peace be multiplied to you in the knowledge
> of God and of Jesus our Lord, as His divine power has
> given to us all things that pertain to life and godliness,
> through the knowledge of Him who called us by glory
> and virtue, by which have been given to us exceedingly
> great and precious promises, that through these you may
> be partakers of the divine nature, having escaped the cor-
> ruption that is in the world through lust (2 Peter 1:2-4).

God is waiting for our commitment to what He has said and provided. The Lord waits for our trust in Him to be expressed through our lives. James 2:17-18 says, "*Thus also faith by itself, if it does not have works, is dead. But someone will say, 'You have faith, and I have works.' Show me your faith without your works, and I will show you my faith by my works.*" Faith must manifest because it is important to God that an individual's response be one of trust in a relationship.

He rewards people with favor when they have faith. This favor seems unfair to others who have not responded properly and are merely spectators instead.

When we verbally thank God and act on what He has done for us through Jesus, He will manifest in our lives in an even greater way. God has a personality, and He loves it when we have implemented the promises of our heavenly Father by faith. Our Father trusts us, and then favor comes that is beyond explanation! God will reward you when you diligently and passionately seek Him daily.

We also need God to show us favor and restore to us what the enemy has stolen. God wants to rescue us if we will only ask and respond in faith. The psalmist said:

> *Please, Lord! Come quickly and rescue me! Take pleasure in showing me your favor and restore me* (Psalm 40:13 TPT).

God has sent Jesus Christ to this earth to redeem us and to display how a Son is to interact with His heavenly Father in two realms. Jesus was the perfect Son and exhibited the traits that we, as redeemed children of the Father, should have in this life. Remember that as Jesus was in this world, so are we (see 1 John 4:17).

Jesus used the authority that the Father gave Him while on the earth. By using the authority of Heaven, He was able to take back what the devil had stolen. Jesus eventually bought back humanity for His Father. The devil has been losing assets ever since because the Holy Spirit is continuing the ministry of Jesus through God's children.

We must passionately seek God and know that He will reward us. I know it is time to enter into the favor of the Lord. Reach out and take what has been given to you in the name of Jesus.

But those who embraced him and took hold of his name were given authority to become the children of God! (John 1:12 TPT)

ANGELIC FAVOR

You have to remember that because our heavenly Father favors us, and because we live by faith and seek Him passionately, as a result God's messengers, the angels, will also know our status and minister to us as "highly favored ones." In Luke 1:28, the virgin Mary had this exact situation occur. *"And having come in, the angel said to her, 'Rejoice, highly favored one, the Lord is with you; blessed are you among women!'"*

The angels know what the heart of God is for your life, and they are on standby to implement favor in response to your faith and obedience to what the Lord has said. Jesus even warned us not to do any harm to children because their angels have access to Father God. *"Be careful that you not corrupt one of these little ones. For I can assure you that in heaven each of their angelic guardians have instant access to my heavenly Father"* (Matt. 18:10 TPT).

We are still God's highly favored children as we passionately seek Him as adults. We have not outgrown our angels as they continue to report to Father God concerning our life in this earth realm.

THE RIGHT THING

When you chose to obey the Word of God in any situation, there is a reward to be given by the Lord as a result of your obedience. It is exciting to encounter favor as a result of doing the works of Jesus. Isaiah shed some light into what God thinks are important actions concerning ministry to others:

Is this not the fast that I have chosen: to loose the bonds of wickedness, to undo the heavy burdens, to let the oppressed go free, and that you break every yoke? Is it not to share your bread with the hungry, and that you bring to your house the poor who are cast out; when you see the naked, that you cover him, and not hide yourself from your own flesh? Then your light shall break forth like the morning, your healing shall spring forth speedily, and your righteousness shall go before you; the glory of the Lord shall be your rear guard. then you shall call, and the Lord will answer; you shall cry, and He will say, "Here I am." If you take away the yoke from your midst, the pointing of the finger, and speaking wickedness, if you extend your soul to the hungry and satisfy the afflicted soul, then your light shall dawn in the darkness, and your darkness shall be as the noonday. The Lord will guide you continually, and satisfy your soul in drought, and strengthen your bones; you shall be like a watered garden, and like a spring of water, whose waters do not fail (Isaiah 58:6-11).

One way to encounter favor, according to Isaiah, is that we must do what is right concerning those who are in need. If we break the chains of bondage, unload burdens, set people free in the name of Jesus and break yokes, then we will have favor beyond our own comprehension.

The Lord, through the prophet Isaiah, continues in this portion of Scripture to tell us that if we will also feed, clothe, and not hide ourselves from people who are in need, that breakthrough favor will come!

BREAKTHROUGH FAVOR

Breakthrough favor occurs when you have acted upon what is on God's heart concerning His revealed will in a situation. He responds with overwhelming favor and deliverance on your behalf. God rewards Christians who diligently seek Him and fulfill His heart's desires for others.

Here is a list of the rewards that are from the Lord:

1. Your light shall break forth like the morning.
2. Your healing shall spring forth speedily.
3. Your righteousness shall go before you.
4. The glory of the Lord shall be your rear guard.
5. You shall call, and the Lord will answer.
6. You shall cry, and He will say, "Here I am."
7. Your light shall dawn in the darkness.
8. Your darkness shall be as the noonday.
9. The Lord will guide you continually.
10. The Lord will satisfy your soul in drought.
11. The Lord will strengthen your bones.
12. You shall be like a watered garden.
13. You shall be a spring of water that does not fail.

We see that God can set you in a place where you will not fail because of *breakthrough favor*. We need to find out what God's heart is and passionately and relentlessly pursue His pleasure! Jesus was just as strong in His belief that it is *rigged in your favor* in the following passage:

Then Jesus gave this illustration: "Imagine what would happen if you were to go to one of your friends in the middle of the night and pound on his door and shout, 'Please! Do you have some food you can spare? A friend just arrived at my house unexpectedly and I have nothing to serve him.' But your friend says, 'Why are you bothering me? The door's locked and my family and I are all in bed. Do you expect me to get up and give you our food?' But listen—because of your shameless impudence, even though it's the middle of the night, your friend will get up out of his bed and give you all that you need. So it is with your prayers. Ask and you'll receive. Seek and you'll discover. Knock on heaven's door, and it will one day open for you. Every persistent person will get what he asks for. Every persistent seeker will discover what he needs. And everyone who knocks persistently will one day find an open door" (Luke 11:5-10 TPT).

Jesus further shows us the reward system and the spoils of breakthrough in His revelation to the apostle John. Jesus proclaims:

"I am the Aleph and the Tav," says the Lord God, "who is, who was, and who is to come, the Almighty" (Revelation 1:8 TPT).

He has everything under His authority if we will allow Him to rule and reign in our lives. He speaks His heart to the seven churches in Revelation 3:13 and then says, *"So the one whose heart is open let him listen carefully to what the Spirit is now saying to all the churches"* (TPT).

There are rewards and favor offered by Jesus Messiah to each of the churches if they will receive His counsel. He is proclaiming that

He will show favor to those who obey what the Spirit is saying and who are passionately seeking Him. They will overcome!

Write in a book what you see and send it to the seven churches: to Ephesus, to Smyrna, to Pergamum, to Thyatira, to Sardis, to Philadelphia, and to Laodicea (Revelation 1:11 TPT).

1. Ephesus

To the one who overcomes I will give access to feast on the fruit of the Tree of Life that is found in the paradise of God (Revelation 2:7 TPT).

2. Smyrna

The one whose heart is open let him listen carefully to what the Spirit is presently saying to all the churches. The one who conquers will not be harmed by the second death (Revelation 2:11 TPT).

3. Pergamum

But the one whose heart is open let him listen carefully to what the Spirit is presently saying to all the churches. To everyone who is victorious I will let him feast on the hidden manna and give him a shining white stone. And written upon the white stone is inscribed his new name, known only to the one who receives it (Revelation 2:17 TPT).

4. Thyatira

To everyone who is victorious and continues to do my works to the very end I will give you authority over the nations to shepherd them with a royal scepter. And the rebellious will be shattered as clay pots—even as I also received authority from the presence of my Father. I will give the morning star to the one who experiences victory (Revelation 2:26-28 TPT).

5. Sardis

Yet there are still a few in Sardis who have remained pure, and they will walk in fellowship with me in brilliant light, for they are worthy. And the one who experiences victory will be dressed in white robes and I will never, no never erase your name from the Book of Life. I will acknowledge your name before my Father and his angels (Revelation 3:4-5 TPT).

6. Philadelphia

But I come swiftly, so cling tightly to what you have, so that no one may seize your crown of victory. For the one who is victorious, I will make you to be a pillar in the sanctuary of my God, permanently secure. I will write on you the name of my God and the name of the city of my God—the New Jerusalem, descending from my God out of heaven. And I'll write my own name on you (Revelation 3:11-12 TPT).

7. Laodicea

Behold, I'm standing at the door, knocking. If your heart is open to hear my voice and you open the door within, I will come in to you and feast with you, and you will feast with me. And to the one who conquers I will give the privilege of sitting with me on my throne, just as I conquered and sat down with my Father on his throne. The one whose heart is open let him listen carefully to what the Spirit is saying now to the churches (Revelation 3:20-22 TPT).

SEASONS OF FAVOR

When you decide to seek God with all your heart, He will be found. God does not hide His face from His children for very long. There is a season to seek Him, and there is a season when you find Him. We have been assured that we will find Him when we seek Him with all our hearts. *"But if from there you will seek (inquire for and require as necessity) the Lord your God, you will find Him if you [truly] seek Him with all your heart [and mind] and soul and life"* (Deut. 4:29 AMPC). Again in the new covenant, Jesus assures us, without exception, *"Ask, and the gift is yours. Seek, and you'll discover. Knock, and the door will be opened for you"* (Matt. 7:7 TPT).

Once a believer is fully convinced of the power of God concerning the blood covenant in their circumstance, they will call out with such boldness and conviction and receive the promises that are given. God is into favoring those who call out to Him. He wants to promote people just as He promoted Enoch: *"he just disappeared from this world because God promoted him"* (Heb. 11:5 TPT).

What about you? Are you willing to abandon your plans and trust God to implement His plans for your life that were written so that you cannot lose? Enoch knew he could not lose because his trust in God became so strong. He continually called out to God for help and became a great prophet of the Lord (see Jude 14).

There is a season of favor upon us right now that will continually cause us to be overcome by God's goodness if we will yield to the move of God's Spirit.

But I keep calling out to you, Yahweh! I know you will
bend down to listen to me, for now is the season of favor.
Because of your faithful love for me, your answer to my
prayer will be my sure salvation (Psalm 69:13 TPT).

Be encouraged by the truth that you are God's adopted and favored child (see Rom. 8:15) and nothing will be withheld from those who passionately seek Him and fear Him. Psalm 147:11 says, "*The Lord shows favor to those who fear him, to his godly lovers who wait for his tender embrace*" (TPT).

I prophesy this word to you now. It is your season for favor, and I smell the rain beginning to fall. I announce, "breakthrough favor now," in the mighty name of Jesus. It's all rigged in your favor!

Your favor will fall like rain upon our surrendered lives,
like showers reviving the earth (Psalm 72:6 TPT).

Chapter 2

YOUR PERSONAL
BOOK OF DESTINY

You saw me before I was born. Every day of my
life was recorded in your book. Every moment
was laid out before a single day had passed.

—PSALM 139:16 NLT

WHEN I WAS WITH JESUS IN HEAVEN, I SAW THAT EACH
person had a book of destiny written about them. It was a
personal book that contained God's heart for us. Each person's book showed how they would affect their generation
and even generations to come. I saw that each book was
conditional, according to how we had allowed our heavenly
Father to implement its contents into our lives by yielding
to His will. I saw that the Holy Spirit was called alongside
us to counsel us into the perfect will of God by moving
upon us in a powerful way.

When I was in Australia, I was ministering one Saturday morning to a building full of people. They had to put seats against the back wall with people even standing at the entrances. All of a sudden, I saw a flash of light and entered a vision. I saw an angel standing beside a couple against the wall in the back. In the natural, I looked over in that direction. The Lord told me to call that couple up and confirm their calling and ministry. So I called them up in front of everyone.

As I laid hands on them, the power of God overshadowed them as I confirmed to them the details of their calling and ministry. When I had finished prophesying, I asked them what was going on with them because the power of God was so strong on them. They said, "This morning we were talking about our ministry and how we needed a confirmation from God. We live on the other side of Australia, so we agreed in prayer that we would board an airplane and fly to Kevin Zadai's meeting in Adelaide. We believed that God would have him call us out and confirm our ministry to us supernaturally." This was a big testimony to all the believers who were there and saw what happened to this couple. They had agreed in prayer, and God answered that prayer within 24 hours. The Lord truly knows what is written in your books and will confirm your calling and ministry if you ask Him.

When I was with Jesus in 1992 while receiving dental surgery, I remember looking into the eyes of Jesus as He was teaching me. I looked right into His eyes as He let me walk right inside of Him. At this point, I watched in a panoramic view the process of me being created. From His heart, a thought of me came up into His mind. As He made an image of me, He then wrote a book about me. The book went to the library of Heaven, and then He breathed my spirit out into my mother's womb. I watched my body being formed inside of my mother until I was born. As I grew up, He was watching over me and I turned out just the way that He thought of me. After I saw all of this happen, I was standing looking at Him again. Jesus just smiled because I was pleasing to Him. I realized at this point that I would live forever with Him because I have faith. Faith causes you to walk according to His Word, in obedience, on this earth. Remember, God Almighty is our eternal home as a Christian so be encouraged when you go through hard times down here on this earth because it will be well worth it.

The profoundness of eternity can be overwhelming when you consider it. Are you ready to live an endless life? God never intended for us to die spiritually or physically. It was Adam and Eve who made that decision as His creation in the Garden of Eden. When we discern the truth that we are going to live forever in the Kingdom of God, we realize that there is no loss.

When I met Jesus face to face, I realized that there were things written about every person who was ever created. Jesus told me that the Father never destined anyone to fail. The Lord explained to me that Father God wanted a family, and when He wrote books about each person, the books were written according to the Father's perfect will for their individual lives. God doesn't write what could happen; He writes His true intention for your life, and that is what you are judged by. God does not write about failure or a permissive approach to what He desires but about His divine plan that must come to pass if we accept it. God's perfect will is conditional upon our agreement and obedience to His will. God calls people to Himself, but few actually answer that call and are chosen (see Matt. 20:16).

We must humbly seek the Lord for His perfect will that is written down in our books. This requires our diligence and will cost us something. We are to truly deny ourselves and follow Him.

Then Jesus said to his disciples, "If you truly want to follow me, you should at once completely reject and disown your own life. And you must be willing to share my cross and experience it as your own, as you continually surrender to my ways" (Matthew 16:24 TPT).

The Lord would have us to pray in the Spirit and meditate on His Word until we can discern the perfect will of God. We will mature into the deep things of God by allowing the Word and the Spirit to take us into our personal book of destiny.

This holy activity of praying in other tongues and meditating on the Word of God is how we are set apart from the world in our daily walk with Him. We must be separate from the world. Romans 12:2 says, *"And do not be conformed to this world, but be transformed by the renewing of your mind, that you may prove what is that good and acceptable and perfect will of God."*

The Word and the Spirit are one. You can allow this mighty sword to rightly divide between the will of God in your spirit and what your own will is in your soul. Human beings have three parts to their makeup in this life. First Thessalonians 5:23 says, *"Now, may the God of peace and harmony set you apart, making you completely holy. And may your entire being—spirit, soul, and body—be kept completely flawless in the appearing of our Lord Jesus, the Anointed One"* (TPT).

Your spirit is the part of you that lives forever and is born again when you confess Jesus as Savior. Your soul is the mind, will, and emotions. Your body is your "earth suit" that you wear in this physical earth realm. Only your spirit is saved at the new birth. As you allow the Spirit and the Word of God to build you up spiritually, there is a division that will occur as the sword of the Spirit separates between what is your will and what is the Spirit's will for your life. The book of Hebrews says:

> *For we have the living Word of God, which is full of energy, and it pierces more sharply than a two-edged sword. It will even penetrate to the very core of our being where soul and spirit, bone and marrow meet! It interprets and reveals the true thoughts and secret motives of our hearts* (Hebrews 4:12 TPT).

Before you were born, a book was written about you and there are truths in that book that will make you a history maker to your generation. Allow the process of revelation to begin to occur by giving permission to the Holy Spirit and by allowing the Word to permeate every part of you. Many in these days are allowing this to happen by letting the authority of the Kingdom rule.

WHAT IS IN YOUR BOOK?

Some people have received the revelation that they were chosen. Jeremiah the prophet was one such person. The Lord spoke to him and said, *"I knew you before I formed you in your mother's womb. Before you were born I set you apart and appointed you as my prophet to the nations"* (Jer. 1:5 NLT). So Jeremiah's book was written beforehand because the Almighty "knew him" before he was even conceived in his mother's womb. It is so powerful when you mediate on the revelation that is in these Scriptures. We are even appointed to our assignment on earth beforehand just like this very important prophet.

In your personal book are written many seasons of blessing and even many seasons of testing—to see what is in you. God is preparing you in the areas where you will rule and reign with Him, not only in this life but in the life to come.

Jesus briefed me on the fact that we are not just down here "surviving" until He comes back for us. We are to thrive and prosper in every area of our life as we yield to His perfect will through His revealed, written Word and by the power of the Holy Spirit.

I felt His glory envelop me and the *"powers of the coming age"* (Heb. 6:5 NIV) strengthen me as Jesus spoke to me during this visit. I am humbled to tell you that what is in store for you is beyond anything you could ever imagine. *"Now all glory to God, who is able, through his mighty power at work within us, to accomplish infinitely more than we might ask or think"* (Eph. 3:20 NLT).

THE DOMINO EFFECT

There is what is known in Heaven as the *domino effect.* Books are written concerning individuals who are "leaned on" by the hand of favor of God and His holy angels. The Lord has plans for you, but those plans involve you influencing those around you in your generation. Jeremiah was so focused on himself and what he perceived as being his personal dilemma. He did not discern how important he was to God's plan for a nation and his generation.

> *The Lord gave me this message: "I knew you before I formed you in your mother's womb. Before you were born I set you apart and appointed you as my prophet to the nations." "O Sovereign Lord," I said, "I can't speak for you! I'm too young!" The Lord replied, "Don't say, 'I'm too young,' for you must go wherever I send you and say whatever I tell you. And don't be afraid of the people, for I will be with you and will protect you. I, the Lord, have spoken!" Then the Lord reached out and touched my mouth and said, "Look, I have put my words in your mouth! Today I appoint you to stand up against nations*

and kingdoms. Some you must uproot and tear down, destroy and overthrow. Others you must build up and plant" (Jeremiah 1:4-10 NLT).

It did not matter that Jeremiah thought he was too young or that he was afraid of the people. The Almighty had appointed him to stand up against kingdoms and nations. His calling as a prophet was to uproot, destroy, and overthrow, as well as to build up and plant.

Now, let's read what happened with the prophet Daniel:

It was the first year of the reign of Darius the Mede, the son of Ahasuerus, who became king of the Babylonians. **During the first year of his reign, I, Daniel, learned from reading the word of the Lord, as revealed to Jeremiah the prophet,** *that Jerusalem must lie desolate for seventy years. So I turned to the Lord God and pleaded with him in prayer and fasting. I also wore rough burlap and sprinkled myself with ashes. I prayed to the Lord my God and confessed: "O Lord, you are a great and awesome God! You always fulfill your covenant and keep your promises of unfailing love to those who love you and obey your commands. But we have sinned and done wrong. We have rebelled against you and scorned your commands and regulations. We have refused to listen to your servants the prophets, who spoke on your authority to our kings and princes and ancestors and to all the people of the land. Lord, you are in the right; but as you see, our faces are covered with shame. This is true of all of us, including the people of Judah and Jerusalem and all Israel, scattered near and far, wherever you have driven us because of our disloyalty to you* (Daniel 9:1-7 NLT).

What is very important to point out here is that Daniel was reading the Word of God that was written by the prophet Jeremiah. Jeremiah had lived almost two hundred years before Daniel was born. As Daniel read the scroll of Jeremiah, he suddenly realized something very important. The prophet Jeremiah had written about him and his people, describing their dilemma of being held captive in Babylon. Daniel soon realized his destiny as he saw himself in the Word of God and so he began to cry out to God in repentance.

Daniel began to calculate the number of years that he had been in captivity in Babylon. He realized that he and his people were over the 70-year mark of captivity. At this moment, the prophet Daniel knew that it was *all rigged in his favor.* He prayed to receive deliverance and restoration back into the promised land of Israel. Here is the exact passage of scripture that was read by Daniel.

> *This is what the Lord says: "You will be in Babylon for seventy years. But then I will come and do for you all the good things I have promised, and I will bring you home again. For I know the plans I have for you," says the Lord. "They are plans for good and not for disaster, to give you a future and a hope. In those days when you pray, I will listen. If you look for me wholeheartedly, you will find me. I will be found by you," says the Lord. "I will end your captivity and restore your fortunes. I will gather you out of the nations where I sent you and will bring you home again to your own land"* (Jeremiah 29:10-14 NLT).

SECRET DESTINY

Here are seven truths that summarize the *secret destiny* that the Lord had planned for Daniel and his people. We can glean a lot of truth from Daniel concerning our own lives. God has truly rigged it in your favor!

1. *You will be in Babylon for seventy years.*

Even though it was not the Lord's will for Israel to be in captivity, the Lord had planned for it to come to an end at a set time. The Spirit of God moved on Jeremiah to write in a previous generation, long before it even happened. God is gracious to us as well, even when we get out of His will. He has set times to restore and deliver us. Your captivity will not last forever when you trust in God.

2. *I will come and do for you all the good things I have promised, and I will bring you home again.*

The Lord promises to come and do only good things for Israel. He desires to bring them home to the land He had given them previously. Remember that your God is a good God. He will not forget what He has promised you. Once you allow the Holy Spirit to lead you into perfect truth, you will see the goodness of God in your life again.

3. *I know the plans I have for you. They are plans for good and not for disaster, to give you a future and a hope.*

The Lord clearly has good plans for His people even in disobedience. He never intended for them to be in captivity or have any encounters with disaster. His plans are for a good future and a hope. We need to renew our minds by the Word of God by allowing the truth of God to transform our thinking, which will enable us to accept a good and bright future. His plans for you are to have a good and expected end.

4. *In those days when you pray, I will listen.*

The Lord promises Daniel, through the prophet Jeremiah, that He will listen to their prayers if they would pray. Remember to pray no matter how you feel at the time. You should always pray—no situation it is too hopeless; God will listen to your prayers.

5. *If you look for Me wholeheartedly, you will find Me. I will be found by you.*

The God of Israel reminds His people to seek Him with all their heart and they would certainly find Him. God, your heavenly Father, will not hide from you forever. He will let you catch Him if you seek after Him diligently.

6. *I will end your captivity and restore your fortunes.*

The Lord proclaims that He will end Israel's captivity if they meet the criteria. Furthermore, He promises to restore even their fortunes. He ends your captivity by delivering you and restoring everything that satan has stolen from you. He has plans for you to prosper.

7. *I will gather you out of the nations where I sent you and will bring you home again to your own land.*

Even though God's people had been scattered to other nations, He promises to gather them and bring them home. Right now, God knows where you are, and He loves you so much that He will come to gather you and bring you back into His perfect will. Just trust in Him now.

> *You've gone into my future to prepare the way, and in kindness you follow behind me to spare me from the harm of my past. With your hand of love upon my life, you impart a blessing to me* (Psalm 139:5 TPT).

Chapter 3

THE LORD KNOWS
YOU PERSONALLY

*Lord, you know everything there
is to know about me.*

—PSALM 139:1 TPT

IN THIS CHAPTER, WE ARE GOING TO BE DISCUSSING the wonderful truth that the Lord Himself knows you personally. It is exciting to know that this truth has been unveiled to us by the Holy Spirit in these days—the truth that we live with the personal touch that God puts on our lives as Christians. A personal touch where God has taken the information that the Mighty Trinity decided before the foundation of the world and has started to implement into our lives.

Isn't it nice to know and to settle within your heart that God understands you personally? Being understood is one of the most important issues with people today. As Christians, we need to understand ourselves as well as each other. It is such a relief when we find someone who appreciates and understands us, and when we spend time with them, they truly know and identify with us. That is the way Jesus was with me when I met Him in my heavenly visitation.

When I met Jesus in 1992, I was going through an operation and He was standing there in the operating room waiting for me. I was outside my body and went with Jesus for forty-five minutes to different places. This near-death experience was so personal to me as I realized that He truly loved me. Jesus' personal touch transferred over into my spirit, and I will always remember how kind He was to me. I also remember discovering that God Almighty has designed everything for me to succeed in life. The books in Heaven that are written about us are good and positive things that are going to happen in our lives. According to our books, we are going to succeed in everything we do. That's the way that God plans it. It's all rigged in your favor!

However, if we want these things to happen in our lives, we must remain diligent because of the evil spirits that will try to come against us. Evil is working against you as well as God. When these evil entities succeed, then you have discrepancies between God's plans for you and what you are experiencing.

I want to make it clear that in Heaven, things that have been written about a person have an expected and perfect end. God has plans for us to succeed, prosper, and to be in good health (see 3 John 1:2). God's plans are based on the foundation that Jesus Christ came back and redeemed humanity. Through the knowledge of the Word of God and revelation that is given to us by the Holy Spirit, we must implement His plan in our lives so there are no discrepancies. I found when I came back from my visitation that it wasn't easy to implement what I now knew, even though I had all the information in the Word of God just like you do.

GOOD PLANS FOR YOU

When you read your Bible, it helps you to know and understand what God has for you. However, if the Holy Spirit doesn't give you revelation while you're reading, then it just goes unlearned. In other words, when I was in Heaven, I saw that the information that we need is always available in the Word of God. However, I also saw that if the Holy Spirit isn't actively involved in revelation and helping you to see and understand how to grasp the concepts, then it just stays on the pages of the Bible. It is the same way when people are talking to you. If you understand what they are saying when they are telling you something, then you say "yes." However, if you don't grasp it, then it goes unlearned, and you can't implement it.

In this life, there are discrepancies because people don't always understand or grasp what God is saying or doing. I saw in Heaven that there are beautiful things written about people—things that they're going to accomplish and the wonderful plans that God has for them to do. However, I also saw that it doesn't always happen exactly how it's written in Heaven because people don't cooperate with God. Additionally, I saw that the angels of the Lord are looking at what God has planned, and then they come down to help people, but they have to get people to cooperate. I'm sure you have seen for yourself how people have their own idea about what God's will is or even their opinion about life. These people seem to be motivated and are moving forward, but unfortunately it's in the wrong direction.

God personally knows and understands each one of us. However, just because someone understands you doesn't mean that they should let you do anything you want to do. If people love you, then they're going to step up and say, "Well yes, I understand you but here is a better way—here is something that you need to consider." And that's the way Jesus was with me. He was just an amazing personal friend, and He cared about me. However, when Jesus told me the truth, there were times when I didn't understand that truth, and as a result Jesus had to correct me.

Jesus had to talk to me and inform me that there were things that I was not comprehending. You have to understand that this may be happening to you as well; they are called blind spots. God is always speaking clearly. However, I realized something about His personality; He will not override our own will. We can work our way into deception by developing this idea that because God personally knows us, He condones everything people think or do. This way of thinking is not the truth. Even though God understands people and knows them, He desires for us to walk in the righteous paths that He has already chosen for us through Jesus Christ. Therefore, the angels are sent down to help all of us get on track. We also need to daily yield to the Holy Spirit who will guide people into their God-given destinies.

Some people may be sent to you by the enemy to plant seeds of fear, doubt, and unbelief into your life, and they're there to work against you. Satan will get people to work against you. He will also try to put people in your life in certain situations to destroy you, slow you down, and stop you. If this happens, it will cause you to miss God's perfect will for your life. So you have to be careful; the angels of the Lord are working on getting you into an environment that's conducive for growth and maturity.

You have to understand that you might not be walking in the perfect will of God because of your lack of understanding or even disobedience. You might just be walking in the permissive will of

God, as it is frequently called. So there is the acceptable or permissive, and then there is the perfect will God. These are degrees of your obedience based on what you know. You cannot do something about a particular area in your life if you do not know anything about it. However, once you do know, then you're responsible for it. Jesus himself instructed me in these areas, and I want to share these things with you because it is essential to understand that your will is involved in everything you do.

God created everything about you, even your giftings and personality, so He understands you inside and out. However, being in certain environments and with certain people can affect your character—the way you act and the way you think. To walk in the Spirit, you have to become, as the apostle Paul said, "separate from the world." You have to set yourself apart because God has set you apart by His Spirit. It was inspiring to see what was in Heaven, but when I came back here, I had to live it out and help people to understand the fact that it is "rigged in their favor" because many people do not get this concept.

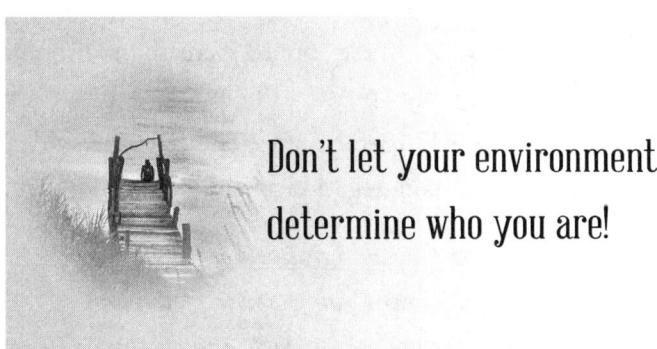

Don't let your environment determine who you are!

When I came back from my heavenly visitation in 1992, I had to learn to not allow my environment to dictate who I was. This process of controlling your environment is one thing the enemy does not anticipate that people will do. He is constantly probing people's borders and trying to get them to compromise by using demon spirits to degrade their defenses. I saw this when I was with Jesus, and it was because of this I did not want to come back! Demon spirits are trained to get Christians to compromise. There is a daily concentrated effort by the enemy to undermine and discredit you so that you never become completely untouchable. Do not allow these demon spirits to win against you by penetrating your borders. Continue to walk in the fear of the Lord and exercise your authority continually in Jesus' name. As you meditate on God's Word, continually placing it before you, you will create borders that satan knows are the righteous ways of God. I saw when I was with Jesus that we are just visiting as Christians down here on this earth and our home is Heaven. We are to walk this earth as priests and kings having authority over every evil spirit, driving them out.

You should never let this world system or the demon spirits of this world dictate who you are in Christ. We are hidden in Christ and the Word of God dictates our covenant with Jesus. Because of the spiritual war on earth, it is very important to walk in holiness and the fear the Lord in this day. Make sure to increase in wisdom, having been baptized in the Holy Spirit and holy fire. I constantly pray the prayer in Ephesians 1:17-23 for myself and for others. The apostle Paul prayed this for the congregation at Ephesus:

> *[I always pray] that the God of our Lord Jesus Christ, the Father of glory, may grant you a spirit of wisdom and of revelation [that gives you a deep and personal and intimate insight] into the true knowledge of Him [for we know the Father through the Son]. And [I pray] that the eyes of your heart [the very center and core of*

your being] may be enlightened [flooded with light by the Holy Spirit], so that you will know and cherish the hope [the divine guarantee, the confident expectation] to which He has called you, the riches of His glorious inheritance in the saints (God's people), and [so that you will begin to know] what the immeasurable and unlimited and surpassing greatness of His [active, spiritual] power is in us who believe. These are in accordance with the working of His mighty strength which He produced in Christ when He raised Him from the dead and seated Him at His own right hand in the heavenly places, far above all rule and authority and power and dominion [whether angelic or human], and [far above] every name that is named [above every title that can be conferred], not only in this age and world but also in the one to come. And He put all things [in every realm] in subjection under Christ's feet, and appointed Him as [supreme and authoritative] head over all things in the church, which is His body, the fullness of Him who fills and completes all things in all [believers] (Ephesians 1:17-23 AMP).

I Can Help

So, this is how I can help you. First, you have to begin each day realizing that it is essentially a blank slate for the day in the sense that you haven't failed yet, because you just woke up. So many things could happen that are wrong during the day, but they have not happened yet. With this idea in mind, the Lord showed me a couple of little things that will help you because He knows you personally. There are certain things that we can do in our daily lives so we don't set ourselves up for failure.

As an example, you know that at certain times you have to be at specific places because you've committed yourself to do a particular thing. So there are people on the other side of this expecting you to show up at a certain time, and after you arrive there's a specific thing that they are hoping you will do. There are commitments that a person needs to fulfill in their everyday life. Therefore, always remember that everyone's schedule is time sensitive and very important. In Heaven it is very similar except it is seasons and events that must happen. God will schedule you in certain seasons as well as individual events. However, sometimes when people begin to move toward those seasons and events, they tend to be late in getting to that appointment. When they get there late, they may encounter a *disappointment* because they missed their *appointment.* Any distance between you and your appointment is called a "disappointment." For example, if there is a gap because you were supposed to be somewhere at 9:00 a.m. and you got there at 9:20 a.m., then it affects others who have certain time-sensitive things that have to happen for you and others.

Remember that people are waiting on you, and it starts a domino effect for your day when you start running late. By the end of the day, you have been just playing catch up all day, trying to get back on schedule. The Lord showed me some things you can do so that you can stay on schedule and not infringe on others who may also have appointments that are important to make in a timely manner.

If you want to walk with God and meet all your appointments, it is going to take discipline. You are going to have to start to be disciplined and be on time. I was trained to be early for everything by the Holy Spirit. Being early instead of on time may take a change in your personality, but it is not right for you to be late. If you've committed yourself to be somewhere at a particular time, you must consider others; it is right for you to commit to doing so, according to Scripture. *"They will speak out passionately against evil and evil workers while commending the faithful ones who follow after the truth. They make firm commitments and follow through, even at great cost"* (Ps. 15:4 TPT).

Concerning someone's personality, someone may say, "Well, that is just their personality." However, the truth is that is not their personality. It is just that they have not been able to discipline themselves to keep their word.

Jesus showed me some things that we can do so that we are not setting ourselves up for failure during our day. Being early is one way we can do that. We need to start thinking ahead and schedule ourselves in such a way that we become consistently faithful, mature people whom others can rely on. Jesus was committed to me when He came and picked me up in the operating room and took me around to different places. He taught me many things while we were in that heavenly visitation. Jesus talked to me about my personality and how He made me a certain way.

IMITATORS OF GOD

However, Jesus shared with me that there were other things that I was doing that were not right—things that were not really part of my personality. He illuminated the truth to me that we need to live a disciplined life. This statement is very significant, so please listen. We have to grow and mature, and when we do, we start to literally act like God. We begin to move as Jesus did on the earth when we are imitators of God. *"Therefore become imitators of God [copy Him and follow His example], as well-beloved children [imitate their father]"* (Eph. 5:1

AMP). We have to begin to learn to be on time and keep our word when we verbally commit to others. Let this understanding become part of your personality. God does understand us, and He knows that it is not easy sometimes to live disciplined, but certain things need to happen in our lives and He has sent the Holy Spirit to help us in our weaknesses.

One of the things that Jesus wanted me to address when I got back to the earth was that each one of us must be an excellent example of Jesus Christ to the world. To an unsaved boss or co-worker, they do not understand when you are late because you initially committed to being there at a particular time. If you're a Christian, your boss knows that. When you are always on time, he considers you faithful as an employee. Be aware that when you are simply on time, it is a good witness for Jesus Christ to the people of the world.

Your personality and who you are as a person comes into play with the giftings of God. The spirit of God will give individual gifts to people. He provides "severally" as He wills, according to the apostle Paul. Those different gifts are attached to your personality. Then you minister as God gives you the ability to minister through your character.

If you see someone yielding to a gift of the Spirit in church, out on the street, or wherever, it might seem a little different coming through them because of their personality. However, it is still the same Spirit and gifting. It is the same thing with the fivefold ministry of the church that Paul talked about in Ephesians 4:11: *"Now these are the gifts Christ gave to the church: the apostles, the prophets, the evangelists, and the pastors and teachers"* (NLT). Through these gifts, we will see unity and a building up of the faith and the Body of Christ to its maturity and not lacking anything.

Although the Holy Spirit flows to others through our individual personalities, we all know that some things that are said and done do not always originate from the Holy Spirit. Sometimes it's just a person's personality, but the gift is still active and it's still working, so don't be discouraged if you feel like sometimes you don't understand yourself. One thing to keep in mind is that your environment and your upbringing has shaped a lot of your personality. Also, the demonic realm sometimes influences your life. They will try to affect your character, but don't be discouraged because God wants to deliver you from all these things.

Your real personality has to do with godliness, patience, and all the fruit of the Spirit, and it's those things that flow out of you that shape you into who you are as a person as well. It is time to get clean of the demonic influences in your environment. Although there may be an influence, we need to stop it now or it will be more difficult for you to undo the way that you execute things in your life. The good news is that the Holy Spirit wants to help you right now. The secret is that when you pray in the Holy Spirit, your spirit is praying but your mind, will, and emotions are not participating in that because your spirit, by the Holy Spirit, is doing the praying to God.

SPIRITUAL EXERCISE

Praying in tongues is a spiritual exercise that builds up your faith according to Jude 20. You are building yourself up in the holiest of faith. According to First Corinthians 14:2, Paul says that when you pray, your spirit prays but your mind is not fruitful; you are not operating in the understanding. Knowing this, you have to submit your personality to be involved with praying in the Spirit. Let the character trait be within you as one who is continually yielding to the Holy One.

The Holy Spirit will have to get a person to the place where they are submissive—yielding and bending toward God and to the things of God. It would help if you said to your mind, "You know this is not an activity that you are involved in. I am praying in the Spirit right now, and you need to be quiet!" The same with your body as it will want to go and do physical activity. When you do something spiritual or a spiritual exercise like praying in tongues, your body is going to want to take you in the opposite direction and you have to learn to say no to its impulses and desires.

Your personality will begin to form by being a little more aggressive and disciplined toward the things of God. We all have to learn to say no and discern that the soul and the body are not cooperating, nor will they want to cooperate with spiritual activity because they can't actually participate in it. They don't have any way of understanding it, so they're going to try to disrupt you and then the demonic will try to come in and also disrupt your soul—mind, will, and emotions—and try to pull you out of the spirit.

Your personality may have to change and be more aggressive, bold, and discerning by yielding to the Spirit. You will need to decide to pray and get in a room by yourself to create an environment where you can pray in the Spirit and not be interrupted no matter what. Once you have done that and built yourself up, then you can go about your day. I have found that my day goes better when I do this. So, you start with a clean slate every morning, and do not do things that set you up for failure. Let God set you up to succeed. It is all rigged in your favor!

Here is my activity every day: I pray and talk to God continually. Let your personal relationship with God go to another level! You do this by building yourself up, praying in tongues. Then, you proceed to schedule your day with its activities and watch how things go so much better. At certain times of the day, you will need to go ahead and yield to the Spirit and pray silently even if you are at work. I have learned to pray in tongues to myself quietly and keep myself in the most holy faith all day long.

I do the same thing during the evening hours. I give some time to praying in the Spirit and meditating on the Word of God. You can build up your discernment by reading the Word of God and getting to know Him on an intimate level. Then you will start to discern that certain things that are being said or done around you are not correct. This activity is an excellent way to finish the day before you go to bed. The important thing is to complete your day meditating on the Lord before you fall asleep.

GOD HAS SOMETHING TO SAY

God wants to speak to you. The Holy Spirit wants to set a precedent in your life by a supernatural encounter. He wants to begin to tell you, "This is the way that you are going to walk, this is where I want you to go, and this is what I want you to say." He's going to start to actively enter your life in a way where He begins to form your personality exactly the way He would like you to be.

There are traits about you that God likes. He put those in you. There are certain things that you may enjoy that are not from God. God has got to be able to tell you if it's not right. Over the years I saw that God started to form my personality into what He wanted. When I was in Heaven, He treated me so beautifully because He had put certain godly traits in me. They were the fruit of the Spirit.

There were things in my personality that He complimented me on because I had been disciplined and allowed God to mature me. Because of that, He said I was known in Heaven. When the Holy

Spirit came on the day of Pentecost, there were many powerful manifestations involved, and that power is still available today. However, you have to remember that this power is coming through a body that is a fallen vessel. The body is still in a fallen state; it's still dying because of the fallen world.

If your soul continually receives information and is educated by the world and not by the Word of God, it will influence your decisions. You're going to have to learn to yield to the things of God until the Holy Spirit walks you out of what you think is right and into what He knows is right. I saw this shift in my life over the years following my experience. I started to discern that there were parts of me that were not correct, and God's personality began to influence me.

When you pray, remember this—when you ask God for something in Jesus' name, remember that God already understands you. He already knows you because He created you. He is personally involved with you through the Holy Spirit to see that you take your next step into your destiny. Well, what is that next step? Remember, the whole goal of the Holy Spirit is to ignite you because He wants to bring you to a holy place, just like every other believer on the earth. It's a place where we as believers dwell in unity and maturity in what we know and do.

Jesus wants to come back for His Bride. We are all supposed to be in unity, believing the same thing, walking in sound doctrine, helping others, and fulfilling the love of Christ. The Holy Spirit continually wants to instruct, help, and encourage us. I saw that the things that are in people's books in Heaven were so much better than what they knew!

God's Perfect Will

I have thought about the books in Heaven concerning my own family. I figured if they would know how it is in Heaven—how things are planned for them—they would understand that His plans are so much greater, and they would enjoy their life so much more. The key is that only through the Holy Spirit could you even know these awesome things. I saw all these things about my family, friends, and about myself. I thought about the fact that I didn't participate in the fullness of what God had for me. The reason was that I had character flaws in my personality that hindered my faith and relationship with Jesus Christ. Someone's personality can be influenced by the system of this world and may not be correct, which in turn prevents them from accepting God's perfect will.

Anyone who would ever go to Heaven and then be sent back to the earth would want Father God's perfect will in their life. That person would say, "You know what? I am finished trying to do it myself and my own way. I want the Holy Spirit to take over and assist me." Nobody who goes to Heaven and comes back would want their way!

I saw that God made everything new in the spirit, but He didn't perfect everything in the soul and body because this earth is in a fallen state. It is a broken system, and satan is the god of it. If you leave things unattended in your life and say, "Well, that's just me," and blame it on your personality or you blame it on your environment growing up, then you have not changed. You have not done anything about the problem. It would be best if you labeled it. In Heaven, Jesus showed me that once you mark and label it, then you immediately start to yield to the Holy Spirit and what the Word of God says concerning these matters. Then you begin to see the Holy Spirit mentor and disciple you in a walk of victory, which is your next step.

Remember when Moses and the children of Israel saw the mountain on fire and received the Ten Commandments? Here you have all these different manifestations happening, but the children of Israel are in unbelief and were still wandering in the desert. When Joshua came forth because he was appointed to take leadership of the people, he didn't just pick up where Moses left off and go around the desert a couple more times. No! It was time to go into the Promised Land. If you read again what happened, Joshua had to fight. He had to go in and conquer cities the entire way up into Israel.

Joshua didn't just wait for God to move. He moved out of obedience, and the Spirit of God gave him the victory the entire way as they conquered all the cities into the land of Canaan. It is the same with you. God wants you to have a spirit of boldness and conquest upon you. That may mean that your personality might have to change a little bit. Your call as a believer includes yielding to the spirit of boldness. Everyone is called to drive out the devil and to lay hands on the sick and see them recover.

That's what everyone's supposed to do. Everyone is supposed to raise the dead. These are all manifestations of the Kingdom of God. For the believing ones who rebuke death, they will see the dead raised. You cannot back off those things. You have to be bold when you proclaim the Gospel.

WHO ARE YOU?

You have only touched the surface of who you are in Christ at this present time. Anyone who begins to have the Spirit of God's revelation about who they are in Christ will cease to be a normal person in this world. That person becomes otherworldly and is delivered from fear. That person is perfected in the love of our Father God and becomes dangerous to the enemy. The apostle John said concerning Jesus, *"But to as many as did receive and welcome Him, He gave the authority (power, privilege, right) to become the children of God, that is, to those who believe in (adhere to, trust in, and rely on) His name"* (John 1:12 AMPC).

This is an amazing statement of truth concerning our relationship with God the Father. We have been given the power and authority to operate in our inheritance as sons and daughters of the Most High God. In *Strong's Concordance*, the word used for "power" is very important to who you are to your enemy. Here is a word study from *Strong's Concordance*:

> 1849 ἐξουσία exousia; from 1832 (in the sense of ability); privilege, i.e. (subjectively) force, capacity, competency, freedom, or (objectively) mastery (concretely, magistrate, superhuman, potentate, token of control), delegated influence:—authority, jurisdiction, liberty, power, right, strength.
>
> - power of choice
> - liberty of doing as one pleases
> - leave or permission
> - physical and mental power
> - the ability or strength with which one is endued, which he either possesses or exercises
> - the power of authority (influence) and of right (privilege)
> - the power of rule or government (the power of him whose will and commands must be submitted to by others and obeyed)

Jesus plainly gave us His authority from the Father God. Jesus commissioned the twelve disciples and then also the seventy to go out and preach the Gospel, heal the sick, and cast out devils. He then said that we would do the same for those were part of the "believing ones." Jesus did not commission only the five ministry gifts to the church, listed in the letter to the Ephesians, to exclusively do the works of the Spirit. These five ministry gifts are the governmental branch of the Kingdom of God and of the church.

The apostle Paul said:

> *And he has appointed some with grace to be apostles, and some with grace to be prophets, and some with grace to be evangelists, and some with grace to be pastors, and some with grace to be teachers. And their calling is to nurture and **prepare all the holy believers to do their own works of ministry,** and as they do this they will enlarge and build up the body of Christ. These grace ministries will function until we all attain oneness in the faith, until we all experience the fullness of what it means to know the Son of God, and finally we become one perfect man with the full dimensions of spiritual maturity and fully developed in the abundance of Christ* (Ephesians 4:11-13 TPT).

These five ministry gifts are to *build us up* in our *"own works of ministry"*! God chose this approach to bring us into unity. The believer who *really* believes is a threat to the enemy. He or she is not stoppable when they walk in love, faith, and unity in the Holy Spirit. Jesus wants all believers to walk in miracles, signs, and wonders. Here is what Jesus said:

> *"And these miracle signs will accompany those who believe: They will drive out demons in the power of my name. They will speak in tongues. They will be supernaturally protected from snakes and from drinking anything poisonous. And*

they will lay hands on the sick and heal them." After saying these things, Jesus was lifted up into heaven and sat down at the place of honor at the right hand of God! And the apostles went out announcing the good news everywhere, as the Lord himself consistently worked with them, validating the message they preached with miracle-signs that accompanied them! (Mark 16:17-20 TPT)

The Lord did not stop with His commission that He gave in the book of Mark. Jesus went even further by the Spirit of God in the book of John. This is where the limitations are taken off of us and we are now responsible for the limitless words of Jesus. He said the unthinkable:

*Most assuredly, I say to you, he who believes in Me, **the works that I do he will do also; and greater works than these he will do, because I go to My Father.** And whatever you ask in My name, that I will do, that the Father may be glorified in the Son* (John 14:12-13).

Now that the plan of God has been revealed, we also discover who we are in Him. Who we are is the revelation that we are sons and daughters of the living God. We are ambassadors of Jesus Christ and we are lethal to the enemy. He knows it is all rigged in our favor as we begin to minister the greater works of Jesus.

I pray right now, Father, in the name of Jesus for boldness for the people. I break the power of the enemy and pray for courage. Lord, all Your people want the personality of Jesus that You gave them. Lord, I thank You for the power of the Holy Spirit's ministry right now in the name of Jesus, and all the people of God say yes and amen.

Chapter 4

GOD PLANS YOUR JOURNEY

You are so intimately aware of me, Lord.
You read my heart like an open book and you
know all the words I'm about to speak before
I even start a sentence! You know every step
I will take before my journey even begins.

PSALM 139:3-4 TPT

IT WAS THE SUMMER OF 1986 AND I HAD JUST FINISHED my undergraduate degree while attending a two-year program in Tulsa, Oklahoma. After completing my first year there and while relaxing at the pool, I fell asleep and had the most amazing dream, full of color, and very realistic. In the dream, I was at the airport in Tulsa, Oklahoma and was walking up to a jet airplane on the tarmac that was owned by Southwest Airlines. The window was open to the pilot in the cockpit, and he stuck his head out and told me that he had heard that I was coming to work for Southwest Airlines. I said, "Yes! I will be hired in two years." Then I turned and walked away. After waking up, I thought that it was a strange dream because I did not want to work for Southwest Airlines as I had other plans to go into full-time ministry after graduating from the school I was attending.

Two years later, when I was ready to graduate, my plan was to travel with the ministry of this particular organization, but the Lord reminded me of the dream and told me that I was going to go to Southwest Airlines. Then, while going to work one day, to my surprise I was approached by the same pilot who was in my dream two years prior! At that time, I was working for a hotel that housed the crew members of Southwest Airlines and the pilot I saw in my dream was one of the crew members that night. I don't recall ever seeing him before the dream and he wanted to know if I was the one who was interested in working as a flight attendant. He had heard that one of the hotel's employees was interested. I told him that at one time I had been interested but now I was going to be traveling in full-time ministry. But the Lord reminded me as I said this to him that I was supposed to work for Southwest Airlines, so I told him that I still might be interested. The pilot then told me that he was going to be in Dallas where the headquarters were located and could check with the personnel manager, whom he knew personally. I gave him my phone number and he called me later on that day from the personnel manager's desk in Dallas. He said that Southwest Airlines was interested in hiring me and needed me to quickly send them an application. I promptly sent the completed application via FedEx, which they received the next day. I got a call from the personnel manager and she scheduled to have me fly to Houston, Texas to be interviewed two days later.

I flew to Houston and was interviewed. Southwest Airlines interviewed 750 applicants that day and chose 33 of them for the position. I was only there because the Lord told me that I would work for Southwest Airlines even though I had no desire to do that! It seemed as though there was a slim chance of even being chosen, so I made light of the situation and thought I would not be selected after the interview. That night I got a call and was told to fly to Dallas, Texas in two days for my second interview. When I arrived, there were one hundred and twenty-five finalists for the thirty-three available positions. As I entered the room, there were two interviewers seated and they told me that I had been chosen. Soon after, I went to training and was hired on July 22, 1988. This was exactly two years, to the month, since I had the dream of the Southwest Airlines pilot!

I remained at that position for twenty-nine years until I was told by the Lord to retire. The Lord has planned out my journey for me, and I am thankful for it. And the Lord has planned out a journey for you as well! It was written down in Heaven that I would work for Southwest Airlines. The airline did so well financially that the retirement alone is sufficient to take care of my wife and me forever because it is all rigged, from the beginning, in our favor.

And it's all rigged in your favor as well, as God has already planned out your journey. However, I want to share with you what you need to do to make adjustments in your perception. The adjustments you need may not be large ones, but they are significant. In other words, the direction of your life will change almost immediately when you do this. It is all hidden in these verses of Psalm 139. Imagine yourself in a timeless realm where there are no clocks and no limitations on distance, so that you can go anywhere very quickly.

It will cost you everything in this life to be in the heavenly realm while you are on the earth, but it is worth it. It would be best if you learned to daily crucify the flesh. The Spirit realm is very fast for us when our flesh does not get in the way. Heaven and the heavenly realms are without limitations. The pre-existent Father, Son, and Holy Spirit were there before time began and before the worlds were even formed. God has always existed; this is an eternal truth that we cannot even fathom. Jesus mentions this in the book of John.

> *And now, Father, glorify Me along with Yourself and restore Me to such majesty and honor in Your presence as I had with You before the world existed* (John 17:5 AMPC).

When I was in the heavenly realm during my dental procedure, it did not matter how long I had been there. What mattered was that I was with Jesus while my body was on a table as the oral surgeon operated on me.

At the time of the operation, although it was essential for my body to have the surgery, it was not crucial for my spirit because my spirit was with Jesus. It was like an entirely different existence while I was in Heaven. There were not the same rules operating in the physical as in the spiritual. Even though my body might have aged while it was on the operating table, it did not age when I was with Jesus, though it seemed like I had been with Jesus for an entire week! You can imagine that God has total control in His realm, and He is not bound by the same limitations that we are bound by. What you need to do is begin to make adjustments in a couple of different areas that I will share with you.

Grasping heavenly concepts is essential for growth. I know you are ready to mature and go on to the next level. The Spirit of God is all about bringing people into the unity of the faith as well as developing them to where they are effective in everyday life. That is what it is all about, and Jesus desires this for you as He experienced this in His ministry on the earth. He saw miracles, but it was because He believed His Father and knew what His Father desired. They were there together from the beginning. Jesus came to earth to redeem us and show us how to walk in the Spirit.

GOD KNOWS YOU INTIMATELY

The Lord is intimately aware of you. He knows everything about you and this is the first adjustment that you need to make in your perception. It is the perception that Father God knows and understands everything about you and genuinely cares for you. It's time to accept this and allow your heart to be touched intimately by His love. When the heavenly Father reads your heart, it is like an open book. You need to understand that the psalmist says that God already knows what you are going to say before you even say it.

The second adjustment is about your words. When you speak, you should talk as though you are speaking the very Word of God that He ordained for you.

> *Whoever speaks [to the congregation], is to do so as one who speaks the oracles (utterances, the very words) of God. Whoever serves [the congregation] is to do so as one who serves by the strength which God [abundantly] supplies, so that in all things God may be glorified [honored and magnified] through Jesus Christ, to whom belongs the glory and dominion forever and ever. Amen* (1 Peter 4:11 AMP).

Jesus said and did only what His Father would say and do. Jesus did not do anything on His own while He was on the earth. That is why in the desert, satan was trying to tempt Jesus to do things that the Father was not doing through Him. In turn, Jesus told satan what God was saying. Jesus gave him the Word back and said no! "It is written!" That's what we must learn to do. We are to speak the Word of God to satan and battle him on God's terms and not on satan's terms. God knows every word we are going to speak, yet not every word you are going to speak will be correct. Furthermore, it is going to take discipline to begin watching your words.

Matthew 12:36 tells us that we will be held accountable for every idle word that comes out of our mouth, and that we will be acquitted or condemned by our words. Jesus confirmed this principle to me. Your words are powerful and we know this from the book of James where the tongue is compared to a ship's rudder with the ability to steer you (see James 3:4). You must watch what you speak with your lips. Jesus said that if you speak to a mountain, believing in your heart that what you declare with your mouth will come to pass, then you shall have it. That is why He said that when you pray, you should believe that you receive. (see Mark 11:23-24).

The third adjustment you will need to make is to know that your heavenly Father hears you. Jesus said, "Father, I know that You hear me" (see John 11:41). Pray to your heavenly Father and say, "I know that You are listening to me right now, and as I ask in Jesus' name I will receive my answer."

Because your heavenly Father loves you, ask what you will (what you desire) and it will be done for you. God wants you to ask Him so that your joy may be overflowing (see John 16:24). As a child of God, our prayers are heard and answered; remember to allow the Holy Spirit to help you.

Jesus told me that as a believer, you should always be talking about where you are going, not where you are. You should not be talking about your condition, but rather about your destiny. It would be best if we were talking about a solution to a problem instead of the problem itself. You must understand that you need to have control over your words. Just because God knows what you are going to say does not mean that you should say something wrong. The Holy Spirit does not stop you from saying wrong words, but you can grieve Him in the process of saying inappropriate things. Everything that I am sharing with you has to do with the journey that God has laid out before you.

As a born-again believer, you have authority when you speak, and because of your God-given authority you should speak wisely. You must have discernment and make right decisions when you talk and pray. Decide that you are not going to talk a certain way because it is not the particular direction that you want to go in.

God profoundly knows your future. He knows everything about you. However, you cannot blame God if things do not work out right because that has to do with you. It has to do with your will being involved. You need to choose your words and your steps by the guidance of the Holy Spirit. God takes over your life through the Holy Spirit and He starts to tell you that you not going to talk that way anymore and that you are going to speak where you are going!

GOD DESIRES GOOD FOR YOU

In Psalm 139:3 (TPT), it says that God knows every step that you are going to take before your journey even begins. This verse means that the whole journey is already mapped out before you even take one step. Think about it this way—you are going to go on a road trip, and the night before, you fall asleep for eight hours. But while you are sleeping, God has already mapped out your trip and knows every detail about it—and you have not even gotten into your car yet! That is what I saw in Heaven. However, Jesus sent me back to talk about how God does plan your journey for you. He already knows what you are going to do beforehand, even though you do not have to listen to the directions for the journey. You can choose to take another route and even get lost. That outcome is not what God plans for you.

God does not plan for bad things to happen to you. His desire and plans are for you to succeed in whatever you do for Him, under the guidance of the Holy Spirit. He loves you deeply and sincerely. He is not working against His children. Jesus went around doing good and healing all who were oppressed of the devil (see Acts 10:38). He was continually healing those who were sick as He traveled from city to city. Why? Because that was what was in the heart of His heavenly Father. Jesus was simply doing His Father's will. God did not make anyone sick. God, the Father, through Jesus, was correcting what was wrong with people according to the heart of the heavenly Father. When Jesus reached out and touched the people with healing power, He was reaching out and correcting what the devil had done. Jesus said, "I am willing to heal, do you believe?" (see Mark 9:23). He was doing the Father's work.

God is doing His work in your life through the Holy Spirit right now. So, you have to resist the devil and begin to discern those things that are happening in your life that are not from God. What are the roadblocks to believing God? What are the things that are hindering you right now?

What is it that bothers you? Trust in God. You will need to label those things and come against them. God knows your journey.

You do not have to make common mistakes. You do not have to take the steps that will cause failure because, essentially, God has already planned out your trip. Your life was written in a book before one day even came to pass (see Ps. 139:16). I want you to start to settle into this truth because this is going to be the shift in perception that changes your life—that God already knows every word that you are going to say, and He reads your heart like an open book.

Let this truth sink in. It might take a little bit of time, but once that slight adjustment is made and it hits you, it is going to shift you so strongly that people are going to notice a change in you. Why? Because people are going to start to hear you talking differently, and they are going to begin to see you doing things differently. Jesus gave me the revelation that He is reading your heart like a book. When you get this revelation, suddenly your next step is going to be one that is from the Holy Spirit's counsel, not from your flesh or an evil spirit. The very words you speak are not going to be from your flesh or your thoughts. They are going to be from your heart where faith is, and you are going to speak from your spirit because a Spirit-filled Christian is going to speak the truth. It is time to speak prophetically and express where you are going. People around you are going to hear you articulate where you are going and see how you walk. When you are out in the world, people notice if you are not like them. You are a Christian, so you should walk and talk like one!

PRAYING THE MYSTERIES OF GOD

Jesus has already read your book. He says, "I have already read your heart and I understand you" (see Ps. 139:3-4 TPT). When hearing His words, you will start to settle into who you are and then you will become bold. You become fearless in the things of God and you realize that people will listen. That is why the devil fights praying in tongues more than anything else in your life because what you are doing is allowing the Holy Spirit to pray out of your spirit inside of you.

The *real you* needs to start speaking. The apostle Paul called it "mysteries in the Spirit." When you speak in tongues, it is articulate and it is known to someone because the language that you speak in tongues is not your language; it is someone else's language. On the day of Pentecost, some people were just bystanders who heard people talking in their language, but the people who were doing the speaking did not know that language. The Holy Spirit wants to pray out the mysteries of God through you. When you yield to the Holy Spirit, you encounter the supernatural realm.

The Holy Spirit is going to help you pray out the book that is written about you in Heaven and then He is going to start to repeat the very pages of your book. The Holy Spirit is going to begin to guide you, but first He will get a hold of your tongue. I saw in the Spirit that He is going to speak out the truth of your situation through *your* mouth. The Holy Spirit needs to be able to pray through you all the time. A Christian needs to pray in tongues all the time. You become a spiritual person because you yield to the Spirit and then walk in the Spirit. You learn to talk and walk in the Spirit because the Holy Spirit takes over. He wants you to trust Him with control of your life. What has been written about you in Heaven is the absolute truth and you do not want anything else.

There is one thing that is going to happen to everybody. It occurred to me when I was in Heaven. I said, "Lord, I could have done so much more for You." I saw that I had everything I needed down here for life and godliness. The promises that were in the Bible were enough to give me victory in this life. I literally had everything that I needed right there on my coffee table and on my bookshelf—the Bible. Additionally, I had the Holy Spirit given to me by the born-again experience and by being filled with the Spirit to overflowing. Those two things—the Word of God and the Spirit of God—were enough to give me victory in life and make me a ruler in the realms of God through Jesus Christ.

When I came back to this earth, I was a threat to satan's kingdom. However, I saw that I had not been walking in the fullness of this revelation. When Jesus sent me back, it took me a while to implement these truths into my life. But over the years, I began to flourish. When I started to prosper spiritually, then I also started to thrive physically and mentally. I began to walk in prosperity and health. I began to succeed in things that I did not understand previously.

I began to do things that I could not previously do. The potential was in me all along, but it had never been released. Why? Because I did not discern what I had. I told Jesus that I would have done so much more if I had understood and known what I had. Then I found out I was coming back, and you can imagine that I did not want to go back to the earth. But the other thought I had was, "This is all rigged in my favor." If I do go back, I already know how it works down here.

Whatever God tells you to do will never fail.

Hearing God's voice is so important in the life of a Christian. We should always do whatever it takes in our life to position ourselves for the voice of the Lord to be heard and understood. I have found from being on the other side of the veil with Jesus that God is always speaking. Because of this, I know that the issue is with the person hearing the voice of the Lord. In other words, it is not the "sending end" that is the problem but the "receiving end," because God's Word is always speaking.

As a believer, one of the most important truths we must comprehend concerning God's character is His faithfulness. God's faithfulness must be grasped and accepted concerning this absolute truth in Heaven that has been established long ago in eternity. Whatever the Almighty God promises, He will accomplish!

> *And he who is the Glory of Israel will not lie, nor will he change his mind, for he is not human that he should change his mind!* (1 Samuel 15:29 NLT)

One of the most special things we have as Christians is a God who wants to communicate with us. It is wonderful to know that God chooses to communicate with us because He created us in His image so that we may sit with Him and talk face to face. Because God cannot lie, nor does He change His mind, He becomes the strength, the much-needed stability in this life within a fallen the world. God would never say something that He did not mean. Everything that the Almighty says He expects to come back to Him accomplished. That is what makes God faithful. He simply keeps His Word to us as dearly loved children.

> *So will My word be which goes out of My mouth; it will not return to Me void (useless, without result), without accomplishing what I desire, and without succeeding in the matter for which I sent it* (Isaiah 55:11 AMP).

This is the absolute truth in Heaven and God will never cease to be faithful. We must meditate on this truth continually until it becomes part of our thinking. It is a response back to Him in an intimate relationship. We should never doubt Him or anything that He has spoken. The apostle Paul told Timothy to wage war with the words that were spoken over him.

So Timothy, my son, I am entrusting you with this responsibility, in keeping with the very first prophecies that were spoken over your life, and are now in the process of fulfillment in this great work of ministry, in keeping with the prophecies spoken over you. With this encouragement use your prophecies as weapons as you wage spiritual warfare by faith and with a clean conscience. For there are many who reject these virtues and are now destitute of the true faith (1 Timothy 1:18-19 TPT).

If what was spoken over Timothy in prophecy was to be used as a weapon of spiritual warfare, then you should do the same. Your verbalization of God's Word over you mixed with faith is a sure thing because whatever God says, He will certainly perform it.

On the other hand, satan does not want Christians rehearsing what was said over them in a prophetic utterance by the Holy Spirit. If we grasped how important it is to engage in this process of the vocalization of prophetic utterances, we would do it more often. The evil spirits who are assigned to hinder and enforce a curse against you must be driven back by the power of the word of prophecy. The apostle John was told that the testimony of Jesus was the spirit of prophecy:

And I fell at his feet to worship him. And he said unto me, See thou do it not: I am thy fellowservant, and of

*thy brethren that have the testimony of Jesus: worship
God: for the testimony of Jesus is the spirit of prophecy*
(Revelation 19:10 KJV).

When we speak forth the truth of God concerning Jesus, the
spirit of prophecy is activated. The Holy Spirit was sent to exalt
the Son of God and Jesus said that the Holy Spirit would testify
of Him.

*But I will send you the Advocate—the Spirit of truth.
He will come to you from the Father and will testify all
about me* (John 15:26 NLT).

We must understand that when we speak the Word of God by
the Spirit of God, we are prophesying. As Spirit-filled Christians,
we are moved by the Holy Spirit to speak and act according to
God's desires. This is a good way to clear the path that God has
chosen for you. We are to be moved by His impulses as He brings
His will to pass in our lives by the mighty Counselor. The apostle
Peter said this about prophecy and Scripture:

*[Yet] first [you must] understand this, that no proph-
ecy of Scripture is [a matter] of any personal or private
or special interpretation (loosening, solving). For no
prophecy ever originated because some man willed
it [to do so—it never came by human impulse], but
men spoke from God who were borne along (moved
and impelled) by the Holy Spirit* (2 Peter 1:20-21
AMPC)

Let the Holy Spirit speak through you as you yield to His
voice. He is waging warfare against your enemy as He accompanies you along your journey. He loves you and will keep you safe.

YOU HAVE WHAT YOU NEED TO SUCCEED

In Heaven, it is set up for me to win and succeed at what God has destined me to experience. It was not like what I had previously thought. Before my trip to Heaven, everything I did had always failed. It was like a setup for failure. I know that some of you feel the same way. That is because the demon spirits that are around you are tripping you up because they do not want you to get any momentum into the realms of God.

Demons do not want you to hear what I am saying and implement it into your life. The evil spirits know that God sends people back from the dead to encourage people to do the right things in life. I know now, after that experience, that the Word of God and the Spirit of God are all that we need. The secret to this life is to take the time to learn how to yield. It is not as difficult as you may think. It is more about discerning the truth that God already knows you and has read your heart like a book.

You can choose whether the next words out of your mouth are going to be a blessing or a curse. You know that you have power and authority in the words you speak. You can choose today what you are going to get out of life. You can pray and ask God for help and He is going to come to help you, but remember that God will expect you to do something with your life because the gifts and callings of God are without repentance.

Can you imagine that God has all these beautiful things for people, and when they get to Heaven they realize that these beautiful plans were available to them, but they did not partake? We will all realize in Heaven that it was not God's fault that you did not seek God and find His plan for your life. Hebrews 11:6 is so essential because it says that you have to believe that there is a God. However, the Scripture also says that a person must believe that He is also a rewarder of those who diligently seek Him.

The second part of that verse needs more attention because we sometimes have trouble believing that God rewards us when we seek Him. Never think that seeking God is wasted time. It is never lost time when seeking God. Part of the problem with many believers is a misunderstanding of God's foreknowledge. You see, even though God knows everything, He does not manipulate you to do what He wants you to do. He is not going to do that. A lot of Christians are waiting for God to push them or to manipulate them into doing the right thing. God is just not going to do that. What He does is this— He gives us His Word and His Spirit, and by yielding to Him we offer Him pure worship.

When you worship God, you yield to Him and adore Him. He is All-Powerful and All-Mighty. He is everything, and we are not. You have to realize that without Him, you can do nothing (see John 15:5). God, in His foreknowledge, is not going to make you do something that you do not want to do. He is not going to make you perform His will if you are rebellious. If a person is going to turn their back on God, He already knows that and is not going to stop that action. The Bible that you own and the Holy Spirit who is inside of you are two things that are available to you every single day. When I died and went to Heaven, Jesus showed me that I was not allowing the Word of God or the Spirit of God to have full reign in my life. He did not have the whole me—only a part of me.

I saw that the Spirit of God was supposed to anoint me to break bondages everywhere I went. God anoints believers so that devils are driven out, sick people are healed, and dead people come back to life. When I spoke, I spoke with boldness to the point where people could not resist what I was saying. I saw that that is the way it was supposed to be. However, I was passive. When you step back and are not aggressive, you are not moving forward. I am encouraging you to start to be disciplined in this area because we are passive, and we do not know it.

TAKE THE BRAKES OFF YOUR LIFE

Jesus sent me back from the dead to tell people that the resurrection power of God in a person's life does not make them passive. The power of God is so strong that you cannot stay passive toward Him. I saw that you have to yield and take the brakes off your life.

By saying yes to the Lord and by saying yes to the next words that you are going to speak, you are taking the brakes off your life. Say yes to the next steps and the Lord is going to help you to finish the way it is written in your book located in Heaven. You do not have to go to hell if you have trusted in Jesus' blood and His redemption. You do not have to go to hell now because you have confessed that Jesus is Lord and you have believed in your heart that He is Lord. When you confessed Him as Lord with your mouth, then you fulfilled what it takes to be born again. You believe in your heart and confess with your mouth that He is Lord; you have given Him every part of your whole life. There should be a manifestation of the supernatural in your life because of Jesus' Lordship over you.

It's the same thing with believing for miracles in your life. How are miracles performed in your life? By yielding to the supernatural. See, you cannot perform miracles on your own. The Holy Spirit inside of you comes out as He manifests through your actions as well as through your words. When you begin to speak the Word of God by the Spirit of God, angels come and stand beside you. They help implement your divine destiny by the power of the resurrection.

When you yield to your heavenly help, you begin to walk in power because you are walking in the Spirit in agreement with Heaven.

These mighty angels will start to embolden you as the Holy Spirit flows out of you with a prophetic utterance. They begin to open doors for you as the Holy Spirit starts to speak through you. Please understand that you are not to be passive. You are not waiting any longer for this to happen. God has already given you the Holy Spirit on the day of Pentecost. When you receive Jesus and you have the Holy Spirit inside of you, then you have all the power you need. The same power that raised Jesus from the dead is living inside of you according to Romans 8 and Ephesians 1. We have the same ability that raised Jesus from the dead!

The eyes of your heart must be more discerning about what you have through Jesus Christ.

> *His divine power has granted to us all things that pertain to life and godliness, through the knowledge of him who called us to his own glory and excellence, by which he has granted to us his precious and very great promises, so that through them you may become partakers of the divine nature, having escaped from the corruption that is in the world because of sinful desire* (2 Peter 1:3-4 ESV).

In his letters to the churches, Paul the apostle wrote about what we have obtained through Jesus' sacrifice. All these things are available to us as believers, but for some reason I did not grasp it fully until I was with Jesus in Heaven. The bottom line was that I did not believe that God rewarded me every time I sought Him. According to Hebrews 11:6, God is a rewarder of those who diligently seek Him.

It is not always easy to miss a meal for God or give of your income. These things belong to you and now you are sacrificing because that is part of seeking God. When we go to church and worship God, we do not always feel like it. That is a sacrifice—a sacrifice that costs you something. We have to believe that God is going to reward us because He does keep track of those things. I also saw this when I was in Heaven. Remember that everything you do for God has been recorded in Heaven. So continue to give sacrificially in every area of your life, because God has planned your journey before you were born and it is beautiful.

The reason why it does not come forth correctly all the time is that people do not understand that it is more about yielding and being led by the Spirit of God. You are like a sailboat—you just need to put your sails up and let God blow through your sails and propel you. It is not like driving yourself in a motorboat. God is blowing you in the right direction. This is what God's Spirit does—He causes you to triumph in any situation. I don't know what it is that you are going through, but obviously God has an appointment with you today and He wants to say some things to you. He is saying, "I have already planned your journey out for you. I know each step and each word that you are going to speak. I have been to your future and it is excellent. I have planned it out and it's awesome."

Now the Lord would say to you, "I want you to worship Me. Submit to Me. Trust Me. I desire for you to yield to Me." That is what He is saying to all of us. He wants us to accept the fact that He is wise. He knows the future and we have to acknowledge our weaknesses. When I came back, it was fascinating to me how I saw that our culture is always encouraging us to be strong. We get to the place where we are talking almost without any humility at all. We are expressing ourselves upward and we are pushing ourselves forward. We are manipulating and presenting ourselves in a way that is repulsive to God. It is part of our culture to push things through all the time.

We all know that if things do not work a certain way, then you can manipulate by getting in there and doing some unethical things and you think that this is a success. If you hurt people on the way up, then that is not God. God is not going to do it that way. The world system does this. God has already planned your journey out, and it's more about just hearing the still small voice of God and letting the Spirit blow into your life as He starts to lead and guide you right now. That is what you want. You want God's perfect plan for you. You do not want to mess it up by running ahead and pulling strings and getting people to do certain things for you.

He has already set it up and the angels will come in to assist. This is why people do not have a lot of angel activity in their life. It's because they are too involved in it themselves. The angels have to step back because you are grieving God. Have you ever heard about grieving God? You can grieve the Spirit of God. He still loves you and you are still going to Heaven, but you can grieve the Holy Spirit. The Holy Spirit has beautiful things for you and things that are beyond what you can comprehend.

However, if you do not yield and accept God's ways, then you are in the way. The Holy Spirit will pull back when He becomes grieved. Often this is something that people do not understand. God is a gentleman in the sense that He will step back and let you have your way because you want your way. But you need to let God rule every area of your life. I tell the Lord that I do not know everything and give Him full authority to do what He wants to do. I have found that when I completely yield to the Holy Spirit in this manner, then my destiny is fulfilled and I encounter greater intimacy with the Lord.

Chapter 5

THE FATHER'S HAND BRINGS IMPARTATION

You've gone into my future to prepare the way,
and in kindness you follow behind me to spare
me from the harm of my past. With your hand of
love upon my life, you impart a blessing to me.

—PSALM 139:5 TPT

OUR HEAVENLY FATHER HAS PLANS FOR US THAT ARE beyond our comprehension. When I was just ten years of age, I received my call to be a mouthpiece for God. One night I was praying in our little Presbyterian church by myself. It was completely dark, and while praying I went into a vision. The Lord showed me the next three segments of my life with each one consisting of seven years. In great detail, the Lord unfolded the preparation that was necessary to accomplish all that I have been called to do. In the vision, at the end of the three seven-year segments, I saw myself back on the mountain of God with my heavenly Father.

Coming out of the vision, I understood very little about what I had just seen, so I did not think much of it. But growing up over the next 21 years, I started to see things from the vision come to pass. Then, at the age of 31, which was the exact year that the three seven-year segments ended, I was on an operating table having my wisdom teeth pulled and ended up encountering Jesus face to face. At this point, Jesus showed me what my ministry was to be for years to come if I chose to go back to the earth. The impartation that I received while I was in Heaven is indescribable. It was as though the heavenly Father Himself laid hands on me. As Jesus spoke to me concerning the Spirit realm and how to operate in it effectively, I realized that ministry was more about yielding to the person of the Holy Spirit in order to be effective.

While I was in Heaven, I was shown a group of people whom I would be sent back to minister to. They each would be signposts along the way as I moved throughout the earth. There would be many people whom I would minister to, but these were just reference points along the way. Jesus spoke to me in great detail about walking in the supernatural power of God in ministry. As He stood speaking to me and teaching me, I thought about the fact that no one had voiced a desire to have His mantle to minister from. I was looking at the exact image of the Father God as Jesus spoke to me. I thought, "I want to have the mantle of Jesus more than any other person." As I looked at Jesus, I saw the Father. I received an impartation during that heavenly visitation that has changed my life forever. I believe that I have the same anointing as Jesus, and so does every minister who truly wants to do the works of Jesus on this earth. The Father God has imparted this to His children through the Holy Spirit by the work of Jesus

Christ on the cross. We receive the Father's impartation when we allow the work of the Holy Spirit to have its full course in our lives.

God is doing some amazing things in people's lives. One key is to know what God is saying to you and what He is doing with you. To fully grasp what God's intentions are for you, you must accept the truth that God has had a wonderful plan for you since before you were even born. This is good news for many people because they have tried their own plans and things are not working out so well. Remember, the Gospel message is good news that you must believe. When you believe, you can receive from Heaven. It is an exciting time that we live in when the Gospel message is being spoken all over the world, telling that Jesus is the answer to everything and that without Him we can do nothing.

Psalm 139:5 says, *"You've gone into my future to prepare the way, and in kindness you follow behind me to spare me from the harm of my past. With your hand of love upon my life, you impart a blessing to me"* (TPT). What a profound Scripture because there is so much in it. Think about this—the Lord who caused you to be born into this world says here that He has gone into your future and prepared a way. Jesus has already walked your path for you! He has already cleared everything out of the way. It is a divine setup because He is standing in your future. I saw this when I was in Heaven with Jesus. I saw that it is precisely as it is written in Scripture. There were things that Jesus said that are also in Scripture, and I discovered that they are absolutely the truth. I realized that I had been in unbelief in some areas. When you are with Jesus, the condition of your heart is revealed and you begin to see that you were in doubt and fear.

This time of visitation with Jesus is part of a process of revelation and discernment. When I was with Him, I realized that many things that I believed were not correct, and many things that I should have known I did not. If I did not know something about a particular topic and did not do anything about it, then nothing manifested. When the revelation came, then manifestation followed. This is part of growing up and maturing.

When Jesus sent me back from this near-death experience, it was so that I could reveal these things to people to show them that there is a proper way to walk in the Spirit and win at every challenge that satan brings their way. Be encouraged, Jesus is in your future as your Victorious Warrior and has cleared the path for you because He has walked on it ahead of you. He will give these things over to you because He knows what is in store for you all along the way.

Protection from Past Hurt

In Psalm 139:5, the psalmist adds, *"In kindness you follow behind me to spare me from the harm of my past"* (TPT). This is profound as God has cleared your future for you. In love and kindness, your heavenly Father goes behind you to where your past is and protects you from the hurt or any harm that your history may inflict on you. Father God is protecting you as a security guard over your life. I saw this to be true. God is not bound by time and He can do a supernatural intervention instantly! God is not bound by anything. Father God is literally in your past, and He is protecting you from it.

Only God can do this. It is a total miracle and I want you to start to grasp the fact that God has already challenged the devil and won in your past, present, and future. Jesus has defeated your enemy, and we must start to believe and accept it. God is enforcing, through a process of revelation, the fact that He has reduced your enemy to absolutely nothing in your life. He has already accomplished that defeat through the cross. Now, Jesus will need to win you over so that you can implement the win against the devil in your own life. The way that God rigs it in your favor is by going forward into your future. Just trust Him and get rid of doubt and fear by being perfected in love. Accept the love of Father God in your life. Love is God, and God is love. In First John 4:18, John says that love drives out all fear. So when you are in perfect love, fear cannot operate. Fear is driven out by perfect love because the Bible says that fear has to do with torment. God does not want any torment in the lives of His children. God has children who are called Christians or believers. As an adopted child, He has bought you and therefore you are now part of the family of God. The devil does not want you to have any of the benefits through being accepted into the family of God.

EXTRAORDINARY PROMISES

The enemy is going to attempt to get you to fear, doubt, and disbelieve so that you will not partake of the precious promises that have been given to you as a born-again believer. I saw all of this when I was on the other side with Jesus. The apostle Peter spoke of these promises in his letters to the churches.

> *Everything we could ever need for life and complete devotion to God has already been deposited in us by his divine power. For all this was lavished upon us through the rich experience of knowing him who has called us by name and invited us to come to him through a glorious manifestation of his goodness. As a result of this, he has given you magnificent promises that are beyond all price, so that through the power of these tremendous promises you can experience partnership with the divine nature, by which you have escaped the corrupt desires that are of the world* (2 Peter 1:3-4 TPT).

The enemy will try to get you to think about the failures that you have encountered in your past, but you should immediately say "no" when he speaks. Say, "I believe and trust God, and I drive out fear." You have to drive out fear by being perfected in the love of God. God's love is being revealed to you by the Spirit of God. He is taking what the Father gives Him and making it known to you. The Word of God is written for us. God did not write His Word for Himself; He wrote His Word for us. The Word of God is a gift from Heaven, the absolute truth that is the foundation of His throne and His surrounding attendants. *"Righteousness and justice are the foundation of your throne. Unfailing love and truth walk before you as attendants"* (Ps. 89:14 NLT). Because the Word has been given to us, we should diligently read and meditate on it. The Word of God is not just pages with words on it. Our heavenly Father has given us the Word as refreshing, living water. Jesus is our bread that came down from Heaven and we should eat of it daily. The Spirit of God is a personal Being and is the third person of the Trinity who cares about you. The Spirit desires to have intimate communion and fellowship with you every day. The Word and the Spirit are always in agreement.

When they come together inside of us, we begin to have a revelation about the Father's love for us. When that revelation comes to fruition, you will know it because the devil will be driven out of your life. When you are perfected in love, you will not fear anymore because there is nothing to be afraid of because you know that God loves you. When you think about your past, you rebuke the devil and you laugh at him because you know that God is standing there according to the Scripture. He is standing there protecting you from your past and so there is no fear. There is no doubt or unbelief in your life because you know God is protecting you from your past. You know He has gone to your future and rigged it so that it is going to work out fine.

God is more for you than you know, and you can change history by yielding to the hand of God.

The amazing benefits that have been given by God through Jesus Christ are not always known by those who are His disciples. This should not be the case. When I was with Him in 1992, I realized that we do not know Him fully as we should. I saw that so much was given, but we did not take advantage of it. My reply to this revelation was, "If I had known all of this, I would have done so much more for You."

However, I should have known! At the time, I realized that I had been given the Word of God, the Spirit of God, and the angels of God. These all have to do with God's ability to help you to be an overcomer in this life. Jesus clearly instructed us to operate in the authority of His Father's Kingdom and be overcomers. Yielding to God's authority and using the name of Jesus will drive out every evil spirit and its work.

Now you understand that I have imparted to you all my authority to trample over his kingdom. You will trample upon every demon before you and overcome every power Satan possesses. Absolutely nothing will be able to harm you as you walk in this authority (Luke 10:19 TPT).

You can see that if you do not yield to the authority of the Kingdom of God and use the name of Jesus, the result will be that nothing will happen. Jesus gave us authority to overcome the power of satan, but if we do not enforce it, we find ourselves being overcome instead of being overcomers in our faith.

If Jesus has clearly obtained for us the many benefits of the Kingdom, then we should discover what those benefits are and yield to the authority of the Most High over us in the Kingdom of God. Part of yielding is this—exchange your inabilities and weaknesses with Jesus' ability and strength. That is why Jesus' name is obeyed by demons when you speak it as a child of God because Jesus is "the name above all names." When a believer announces the name of Jesus, he or she accesses the authority of the highest possible position and Person who inhabits eternity.

> *You must have the same attitude that Christ Jesus had. Though he was God, he did not think of equality with God as something to cling to. Instead, he gave up his divine privileges; he took the humble position of a slave and was born as a human being. When he appeared in human form, he humbled himself in obedience to God and died a criminal's death on a cross. Therefore, God elevated him to the place of highest honor and gave him the name above all other names, that at the name of Jesus every knee should bow, in heaven and on earth and under the earth, and every tongue declare that Jesus Christ is Lord, to the glory of God the Father* (Philippians 2:5-11 NLT).

There is a revelation of His glory and power that will cause you to operate in your future at the present time. There are no limitations being put on you in the realm of the Spirit. You are well able to side with Almighty God and His desires for you as you let Him implement the best plans that He has designed for you to come to pass. He wants to use you to be a history maker in your generation. When you yield to the Holy Spirit and the angels, the Word of God that has been written and spoken will become reality and change the course of history. In Heaven, the books will show that you did mighty exploits by the Spirit of God in this life as many people will turn to the Lord and repent and be saved.

Become a partaker of the divine nature of God. Our loving heavenly Father has given us the ability to have so many encounters for the purpose of knowing Him. His goodness and glory are being manifested continually. We don't have a thing to worry about as we begin to explore and discover God's many benefits through Jesus Christ. These benefits have been bestowed on us through partnership with Him. God Himself will enforce the blessing in our life, and we will encounter His amazing power.

> *Everything we could ever need for life and complete devotion to God has already been deposited in us by his divine power. For all this was lavished upon us through the rich experience of knowing him who has called us by name and invited us to come to him through a glorious manifestation of his goodness. As a result of this, he has given you magnificent promises that are beyond all price, so that through the power of these tremendous promises you can experience partnership with the divine nature, by which you have escaped the corrupt desires that are of the world* (2 Peter 1:3-4 TPT).

We have a divine deposit within us that gives us access to the divine nature with His hand upon our lives. We are called to walk in a "glorious manifestation of His goodness."

HIS HAND OF BLESSING

At the end of Psalm 139:5, it says, *"With your hand of love upon my life, you impart a blessing to me"* (TPT). It is so good to know that God does not want to curse us. He wants to bless us. He wants to lay His hand on you and impart to you a blessing.

Every day we receive another breath, we receive our health, we receive all these benefits, and we should thank God for it. We are receiving from Heaven all the time, but Father God also wants to impart a blessing to us. How does He do that? In the Old Testament, they used to lay hands on people. They would transfer a blessing or an anointing onto the next person. In the case of a patriarch, it was Abraham who imparted to Isaac and then to Jacob, and we have the history that goes on from there. Joseph went into Egypt and then Moses went out with the children of Israel. The history continues into Canaan and the land of promise. There is impartation to Isaiah the prophet. His impartation from Heaven was written down, and we have the Word of God from what was given to him from Heaven.

We have the prophets—Elijah, who was imparted with the anointing to be a prophet to the nations. Then from Elijah came Elisha, who got a double portion and then operated in double what Elijah did. It is the same way when Jesus imparts a blessing to the twelve disciples. From those twelve, we got seventy who went out and healed the sick and cast out devils. Jesus had the three—Peter, James, and John—who were very close, and it continues.

On the day of Pentecost, there were one hundred and twenty, and that turned into three thousand people in the church in just a very short amount of time. It just kept growing and growing and growing from that point; that is impartation. In Deuteronomy 28, God gives a choice of whom to serve and obey. He said that you can choose a blessing, or you can choose a curse. It was more about obeying what God had said and discerning that He is God. He says that if you keep these things before you and follow them, these blessings are going to come upon you. However, if you choose to not follow and obey God, and if you do not keep them before you, then these curses are going to be upon you. Then He told them, "Choose this day which ones you want." So we have the right to choose what we want. Do we want blessings or curses? When Father God says, "Listen, I am going to impart a blessing to you and put My hand of love on you, and I am going to bless you," that is favor! God has decided that He is going to take what is His and put it on you. To paraphrase Psalm 139:5, God is saying, "Not only do I know your future and have gone ahead of you to make your path clear and straight, but I have also gone behind you, into your past, and there I protect you from the harm of your past. I am going to impart a blessing upon you by laying My hand upon you, and you are going to be favored."

THE PERSONALITY OF GOD

The blessing is so substantial because it is part of God's personality. God is transferring by putting His hand on you. As His child, you receive that impartation and what you need begins to manifest in your life. Your body responds and you start to see healing. Your soul begins to heal as your thoughts and emotions are affected. With the blessing of Father God, you begin to sense a change in your spirit. You have abilities that are beyond what you had before. Spiritually, you start to walk in areas of the supernatural that you have never seen before!

I believe in these last days that you are going to start to see miracles where people are walking with God as Enoch did. These believers will do extraordinary miracles. Some things will not be able to be explained. It will just be God's goodness expressed through uncommon favor. That is the favor of God that cannot be explained. God is imparting His love for a person, and that love turns into a blessing. Our body, soul, and spirit respond to the blessing. Everything you touch and say starts to prosper and you begin to have supernatural abilities. It's because the Father's hand is upon your life. No earthly father would not want his children to have everything that they needed or desired. Every earthly father would want their children to do better than they had done. They would sacrifice everything they could to make it an environment where their child would excel.

You know that no child would be neglected under Father God's care. There is a process of informing people as to what the Word of God says. One of the things I was shown when I was with Jesus was that people do not have the Spirit of revelation, so they are unable to daily walk in it. It is fascinating to me how there is a great focus on the Holy Spirit and yet we still do not understand Him. This lack of understanding is because we do not know how to yield to Him who is the "Spirit of Revelation" (see Eph. 1:17). That is the reason why we miss God's perfect will sometimes.

Among believers, there is also a great emphasis on Jesus, and yet we do not fully understand the truth that we are co-laborers with Him. We don't comprehend that we are fellow servants, brothers, and friends of Jesus. At the same time, He is our Savior, God, and the Head of angel armies. There are many different roles that Jesus fulfills. However, we do not understand everything there is to know about Him and do not grasp His different roles in our lives. The more we understand, the more we will see supernatural manifestations in our lives.

The Father is not revealed except through the Son (the Word) and Spirit and so there is a lack of understanding in this area of our heavenly Father. I saw this when I was in Heaven—that people do not fully understand and know Father God. Most believers know the Holy Spirit and Jesus. Moreover, I found out that many people think they understand the Trinity, but the Father is a mystery to them. Even when I was in Heaven at the throne room, the Father was so mysterious to me. At that time, I knew Jesus and I knew the Holy Spirit, but I realized that the Father was hidden. He never really revealed Himself outright. The Father uses the Holy Spirit and the Word of God, who is Jesus, to reveal Himself.

THE FATHER REVEALED

In the coming days, I was told that Father God is going to be revealed. I saw that there is a part of God called the "glory of God." The glory is the personality that comes out from God the Father that fills the throne room, and Jesus is part of this. The throne is surrounded by this glory, and I saw that in the last days the glory will come into the church and be manifested in different places of meeting and there will be a revelation of the Father coming forth.

What is it that you need in your life right now? What is it that is lacking in your life? I found out that a lot of what we go through in this life is because we do not understand. We do not have the revelation of what a proper father should be. Today, this is a device of satan. It was revealed to me that satan wants to rob us by making us a fatherless generation. A Christian has been given the authority to break the powers of the enemy and to walk in victory in this life. The person who does not have the born-again experience will have no resistance against evil spirits and the god of this world.

Paul said that before you were born again, you did what the spirit of the world told you to do and you had no resistance to the god of this world (see Eph. 2:2). When I was in Heaven, this resounded in me. I saw where people could not be good parents because the enemy's presence in this world fights people so much that children grow up not knowing what it is like to be loved unconditionally by parents—especially fathers.

Fathers are an authority figure. You need a revelation about authority and about how to handle situations. We do not walk in that authority because we have not had a revelation of the Father. In these last days, there is going be a shift of more emphasis on Father God. You will see revelation come forth through teaching where we will see the Father's heart. God is going to come forward in the Father role in these last days and start to reveal Himself. He is going to begin to visit our services in the glory cloud. We are going to begin to see more healings in our services, because when the Father shows up and the glory comes in it affects people's bodies and causes healings to accelerate. You are going to start to see teachers becoming fathers. You are going to have discipleship going to another level in these last days. People will no longer be students only, but they will be disciples.

There is a difference between teaching and discipling. When someone teaches a person, they are informing and educating them. A disciple is when you have a master who is discipling people and replicating themselves into their students. And this is what I am called to do. You can teach people, but the student might not receive a transfer through impartation to carry on to the next generation. If you want to transfer and impart, you must disciple others.

Disciples will walk in what you are walking in and that is what happened with Jesus. His disciples were supposed to do what He could do. When something would go wrong, people would come and complain to Jesus and say, "Your disciples could not cast out the devil; they could not cure the person" (see Matt. 17:16). Jesus asked His disciples how long He would have to be with them. The reason why He said that was because He was trying to impart into them and replicate Himself in them so that they could do it themselves.

That is why Jesus said there was coming a time when the Holy Spirit's arrival would bring greater works than what He had done. In John 14:12, He said, "He who believes in Me, the works that I do he will do also." Then He said, "and greater works than these he will do." The disciples were thinking about how they could not even do what Jesus was doing, let alone greater works. This whole idea was coming from the Father who wanted to replicate Himself in people. Christianity and the entire notion of having a church, having an education, having Bible studies, etc., should not be to simply inform people of truth only, but to take it another step as Jesus did. The Father was working through Jesus to replicate Heaven and replicate Himself, and this is what Christians should also do.

Father God wants to take you into what He walks in and what He knows. That is what Jesus did with the disciples. In three and half years they did not get it, but then eventually you can see in the book of Acts where they all started to walk in it. That was because it began to take root. All the time that Jesus imparted to them and prayed for them, it all started to take root. In the book of Acts it says that they took note that these disciples had been with Jesus (see Acts 4:13).

The people of that day saw when believers began to act like Jesus. They saw the faith, the miracles, and the Word of God being preached with boldness. They started throwing them in jail to try to stop them because they had become very potent and had become a threat to the enemy. That is indeed what the Father's heart is for you. He sent me back so that I could replicate what God is doing in my life into others. My purpose is to transfer and impart this to you because that is what God wants.

He wants each one of us to walk in this. You can trust the Word of God. You can trust the Holy Spirit inside of you and walk in miracles every day. You can do this; the idea of a father imparting to you is coming back to the church. Paul said that we have many teachers, but we do not have many fathers (see 1 Cor. 4:15). Paul was trying to say, "Look, I got thrown in jail so I cannot be with you right now, but I am jealous over you because other people are coming in who are trying to take you away from me."

Paul was jealous over their relationship and God is a jealous God and jealous over you. He wants you for Himself. Father God is going to impart to you. However, when He does He wants you to start to act like His Son Jesus. On the earth, we are going to be like Him in this world and you are going to begin to see miracles. When I started praying from this revelation, it started to get stronger and I began to see the answers coming quickly. I had to be careful of what I asked for because I was getting it. I started to say things and then, in turn, I began to see things that I had prayed for in the name of Jesus.

Father, in the name of Jesus, I thank You for the impartation from Your throne. I bless each person in the name of Jesus, and I break any powers of the devil over them in the name of Jesus. I thank You, Father, for victory. I thank You for an impartation from Heaven. You love them and are driving out all fear in the name of Jesus.

Chapter 6

HIS SPIRIT GUIDES YOU

Wherever I go, your hand will guide me;
your strength will empower me.
—PSALM 139:10 TPT

I REMEMBER SHORTLY AFTER I WAS BORN AGAIN, I attended a Bible study that was affiliated with a church that believed in both the born-again experience and the Spirit-filled life. The Bible study group was held in a member's house and consisted of mostly the youth of the church. It was so good for me to be around people who believed the way the Bible taught, unlike my previous church that did not even believe in the born-again experience.

Each Monday night when the meeting started, the leader would ask for any special testimonies that had occurred during the previous week or something that the Lord had shown one of the attendees that could be shared with the whole group. I would wait for someone else to share, but usually no one did. I always had something to share because the supernatural was working in my life on a regular basis, even as a new Christian.

After a few weeks of sharing with the group the things that the Lord was doing in my life, the leader pulled me aside and let me know that this could not be happening with me because I was a new Christian. He let me know that he was a more mature Christian and was my leader. He stated that God would not be speaking all these things to a newly converted student. In other words, God would speak to him first and not to me.

This leader spoke that to me with all the attendees listening. I then went into an open vision and was suddenly standing outside the house on the sidewalk. I could not see anything inside the house while I was in this vision. I heard the audible voice of God speak to me and tell me to look down at the sidewalk that I was standing on in the vision. The Lord said, "Pick up the wallet that is in the grass edging of the sidewalk." I looked down at the edge of the sidewalk where the grass was, and to my surprise there was a brown wallet lodged between the cement and the grass.

At this point I came out of the vision and could hear the leader continuing to correct me. I was now back in the house and did not understand what had just happened to me. I immediately picked up my things and left and went out to my car. I found the spot where I had just had the vision and looked down and there was the wallet. The Lord told me that it was my leader's wallet and that I should pick it up and take it to him as proof that I was being spoken to by the Spirit of God and that he was wrong in judging me.

I immediately picked it up and walked into the house, opening it so that his driver's license was visible to show him. When I handed it to him, he was in shock. He wanted to know where I found it, as it had been missing for three days. I told him that while he was scolding me, the Lord spoke to me and told me where his wallet was, so I went and got it. The Lord told me to never go back to that Bible study again. I tell the story to encourage everyone that God wants to lead you by His Spirit. It does not matter how young or old you are in the Lord. We all have the same Holy Spirit as Christians and have the same opportunity to be led in a powerful way.

THE SPIRIT GUIDES YOU

It is exciting to discuss the intricacies of how the Spirit of God works with us as human beings. We are starting to learn about the fact that we are spirit beings and not just physical or psychological beings. We are to walk in the Spirit. It is essential to keep your body disciplined and your mind educated so that they are trained to not fight against your spirit. God never intended for the body and the mind to rule you.

When I came back from Heaven, I realized that the most essential part of us is our spirit. I realized that the born-again experience literally makes us a new creation in Christ, one that has never existed before. The born-again experience then accelerates you into the world of the spirit, which means that you can now have supernatural events happening in your life all the time because your spirit is a supernatural part of you. The Spirit of God guides you in your spirit. He guides the spirit part of you—your spirit man, your heart, the part of you that became born again.

When the Spirit guides you, He leads you into all truth within your spirit; it is spirit to spirit. God is not a body and He does not have flesh as we do. He is not going to talk to us through our flesh.

He is not just a mind or a brain and He does not only have emotions. God is not going to appeal to your feelings because God is a Spirit.

God is Spirit, and those who worship Him must worship in spirit and truth (John 4:24).

SPEAKING SPIRIT TO SPIRIT

God is a Spirit, and He talks to you through your spirit. It is all "rigged in your favor" because God went to the very heart of you, placed His Spirit inside of you, and then He speaks to you from there. If we really knew all of this, we would not have the problems that we have. It is the fact that we do not understand how we were made and how God deals with people; He deals with people in their spirit. God is going to get to you in your heart first. He is not going to send people to speak to you and convince you in your mind that you need to make decisions. Angels will sometimes manifest themselves in a pure physical form because that is their last-ditch effort to get your attention. We can be led by angels and never see them. There are always angels around you. I don't know if there's ever been a time when there are not angels somewhere around me. Everyone has angels, and God is leading every Christian to some degree. Christians are not always aware of their spiritual surroundings.

In Psalm 139:7-10, the psalmist says, *"Where could I go from your Spirit? Where could I run and hide from your face? If I go up to heaven, you're there! If I go down to the realm of the dead, you're there too! If I fly with wings into the shining dawn, you're there! If I fly into the radiant sunset, you're there waiting! Wherever I go, your hand will guide me; your strength will empower me"* (TPT). I want to focus on verse 10, where it says that no matter where you go, God is going to be there. You cannot run or get away from God. Wherever you go, and whatever direction you decide to go in at any one moment, He is there waiting for you.

You can resolve this truth in your heart by accepting the fact that you cannot get away from God. This also means that you cannot get away from who you are and what your calling is. You cannot run from God. Some prophets in the Bible tried to get away from God and from the calling of God. They found that they could not, and that God would not let them go because the gifts and callings of God are without repentance. In other words, it is not up to you. God has chosen you to do certain things. If you are going to be a Christian, and if you want to follow God, then you turn yourself over to Him; that is part of being a Christian.

The apostle Paul said that the life he lived was not his own. He even said that your body is the "temple" or the "house of God"—that it is not your own anymore (see 1 Cor. 6:19). This truth seems to have lost its place of importance in our lives. I have watched it slip in the last couple of years, as people are not acknowledging that God owns their body, mind, and spirit and that their life is not their own. You now have to let Jesus live through you. He is continuing His ministry through you as a Christian!

Everyone is a minister, and everyone is going to yield to Jesus. He is going to live His life through you. He is going to take your body over to express Himself. It is all about manifestation. You have to yield to revelation if you expect to see the manifestation of that revelation. Once you receive the revelation, you will then receive the visitation and then the habitation. By His Spirit, God is taking you on this journey and revealing Himself to you by showing you His ways. The Word says that Moses understood God's ways, but Israel only saw God's acts (see Ps. 103:7).

ENGAGE WITH GOD

I don't want to be a spectator. When something contrary would happen, the Israelites would get afraid and they would not engage God in a personal manner. You need to engage God in a personal manner, which means you are going to have to really get to know Him. By knowing Him, you will engage Him on His terms. When people truly know God, they do what He asks, and they do not question it. I am not living my life in such a way to try something to see if it works. I wait on God until He tells me what to do, and then whatever the Word of God says, I do it. I am not waiting for God to confirm it. It is already written and that is the way it is.

In Psalm 139:10, it says, *"Wherever I go, your hand will guide me."* You should see that there is no place to go that we are away from Him. He mentions hell and Heaven. He says that He knows every direction that we go. As soon as we get there, we are going to encounter God. We cannot get away from Him because He is the center of all creation and not bound by anything except His Word.

Wherever you go, He is going to guide you. What does this mean to you now? You have to hear His voice. You have to follow what He is saying. When He comes upon you, the hand of the Lord will guide you. He will show you or put you in the right direction. It is intimate to have God's hand guide you as it says here—it is describing intimacy.

I can feel the hand of the Lord on me, and it is so sure that I do not have to ask any more questions. I know the direction that God is telling me to go, but that was over years of getting to know Him. I did not always understand God that way, but I was willing to learn. When you are eager to yield to the Holy Spirit and let yourself go, God will start to rule and reign in and through you. Let God dictate what you do and what you say. He has a better way than your approach. You have to learn to yield and say, "Lord, You know what I do not know." It is time to fully trust Him.

As soon as you say that you trust Him, it is recorded in Heaven, and God and the angels know that you have made that commitment. It means that you are going to become more intimate with Him. He can trust you with what He has for you. Your heavenly Father is going to bring you into this special place of empowering you. He is going to strengthen you as the Scripture said. When His mighty hand comes upon you, He is going to guide you, strengthen you, and empower you.

I think about the Holy Spirit coming upon me in the early days after becoming born again and filled with the Spirit. The power of God strengthened me and led me. I regularly saw miracles happen. I encountered the supernatural even in the times when it was hard, and God was there for me. When the hand of the Lord comes upon you and He starts to touch you, your life starts to shift and change. It has to do with the fact that you see things differently.

You are yielding to His guidance and His power. Then the touch of His hand starts to rub off on other people around you. In the first stages, He answers your prayers when you seek Him. When He does come, He is going to shift your reality and the way that you perceive things. He is going to lift you up and put you in a place where your vantage point is going to be on a higher ground. You are going to see things you have never seen before. You are going to understand things that you could not figure out before.

When you begin to do what God has told you to do, it is going to succeed, and it is going to seem so natural. That is because He is strengthening you and working with you while guiding you; that is what the psalmist was saying. You are about to be ushered in to your next phase of intimacy with Father God. Receive your empowerment now. The walk in the Spirit can be mighty and can be very intricate and detailed because it matches the books that are written about you in Heaven.

I know that you want what God has for you. You cannot just wait for things to happen by themselves; you have to allow the Spirit of God to implement those things into your life. Be a doer of the Word and one who speaks where they are going. Speak to your enemy and to the mountains that are before you and tell the Lord that you believe His Word and do not have any doubt.

> Listen to the truth I speak to you: If someone says to this mountain with great faith and having no doubt, "Mountain, be lifted up and thrown into the midst of the sea," and believes that what he says will happen, it will be done (Mark 11:23 TPT).

The manifestation starts to happen as He guides you. Then revelation will flow through your heart, which then becomes a powerful word out of your mouth. You cannot just leave it as a revelation in your heart. You have to begin to speak it. After you have spoken it, your vision will become apparent, your hearing will become clear, and then your feet will start to walk it out. You will begin to do it. It is not just a thought anymore; it is a deep knowing that comes out of your mouth in words, and then your feet start to walk toward what you have spoken. This is the plan of God for your life.

COMPEL THE PEOPLE

Ministry is all about allowing God to do the works of Jesus through you. Jesus is still ministering on the earth. I hope you know that His ministry has continued even after His body left because now we are His Body. We are the Body of Christ as believers, and we all have our own part to do for Him. Jesus is just fulfilling what He did in the spirit realm at the time He bought us back and went to the right hand of God.

Jesus is fulfilling His ministry through us. Paul says in Second Corinthians 5 that we have a ministry of reconciliation, and we are to go out and encourage people to come to Jesus and share with them that the price has been paid. We are to tell people about the Good News of Jesus Christ and encourage them to come in and accept the Lord. It is as though Jesus Himself is appealing to the lost through us. This is ministry and this ministry is for everybody. You do not have to be in a specific position in the body of Christ—an apostle, prophet, pastor, teacher, or evangelist. Everyone is called to the ministry of reconciliation.

The five-fold ministries are all critical as God has designated them. However, the believer is very powerful—simply because he or she is a believer in Jesus. Not everyone is part of the five-fold ministry. As a believer, you can still be a minister under the power of the Holy Spirit, and you can always do the works of Jesus. He said that these signs should follow those who believe, and the Scripture goes on to describe casting out devils, healing the sick, preaching the Gospel, and even raising the dead (see Mark 16:17-18). These are mighty manifestations of the Gospel that every believer can walk in.

You do not need to have a special calling or an individual office in the church to do these things. You can be a believer. Remember, God's hand is on you, and when He comes to you certain things are going to come out of you for His glory.

Jesus Working Through You

When you go through hard times, you have to realize that it is warfare that is going on and evil spirits are trying to slow you down. God calls you, chooses, anoints, and gives you instruction in the Word of God. He gives you the Spirit of resurrection power. The Holy Spirit wants to minister through you. But He has to get you out of the way. There is a time that comes when people want the hand of the Lord on them. They want to be led by the Spirit, but they have trouble, and they want to know why there is so little activity in their life. They want God to move and want Him to do things.

I will tell you what it is. It is a fact that people are waiting for God to do it. They do not allow God to do it through them, and instead they try to imitate. Just like a person can train a parrot to talk. You can train the parrot to say something and then the parrot will say it. It sounds like he knows what he is saying, but the parrot really does not understand what he is saying. The parrot only hears sounds and repeats them but has no understanding of what he is actually saying.

There are certain Christians who do nothing. They sit and wait, and if God wants to move, then He will move. If He does not, then He will not do anything. So, nothing ever happens because God is waiting for them, and they are waiting for God. On the other hand, you also have Christians who will go ahead of God and will try to make things happen when it is not the Spirit of God. You must have a balance. You have to be able to sit back and listen to what the Spirit is saying and be willing to act, and know the difference between your voice and the Holy Spirit's voice.

God wants to guide you, but what I saw when I was in Heaven was the fact that people do not live a crucified life. They do not deny themselves, pick up their cross, and follow Jesus. Instead, they get saved because they do not want to go to hell. When they make the decision that they do not want to go to hell, then they accept Jesus because that is the way out of that process. They get saved because they want Heaven, and they do not want to go to hell and that is obviously a good thing. However, the problem with that is in the rest of their life they are just happy that they made it in and they do not do anything else with their spiritual growth, and that is not a good thing. When I was in Heaven, I saw that you get rewards for what you do with what you receive in this life.

You cannot just sit on your gift and bury it in the ground. The parable that was given in the Bible by Jesus showed that the person who hid his money and did not invest it also did not get a return on his talents. That man had his taken away from him and given to someone who did the right thing (see Matt. 25:14-30). In Heaven, I saw that there are Christians who wait and wait and wait for God to do something, and then they complain when nothing happens, and then they say, "It does not work."

Then there are the people who go ahead of God, who manipulate, push things, and try to get things to happen, but they do not know God. It becomes like that parrot—they start saying things, but they do not believe it. They are just saying it, thinking that if they say it over and over again it is going to happen. Some people do it to bother God to the point where they think, "Well, if I keep asking Him, He is going to give it to me, even though He might not want to. He's going to give it to me just because I keep bothering Him." This is not a relationship. You know, God does not want you harassing Him all the time. He loves you. Your heavenly Father desires to have a relationship where you can just come and ask Him once. You can ask God once in faith, and you never have to mention it again; it goes down as a request, and He answers. God will answer all your prayers; that is the bottom line.

When you are dealing with your walk with God, you have to remember this verse in Psalm 139. Remember that His hand is going to guide you wherever you are. The psalmist says that even in the realm of the dead, God is also there. God is always with you. God takes you by the hand, puts His hand on you, and that hand influences you to walk in the depths of God, in the power of God, in miracles, and in the supernatural. It gets to the point where Jesus starts to invade your financial realm, your physical realm, and your mental realm. He gets into your job, into your career, into your marriage, and into every area of your life, and He begins working in and influencing those areas. That is the step that the Holy Spirit wants to take with you. However, you must be willing to crucify your flesh, deny yourself, and follow Him.

Jesus said that if you leave everything for Him—houses and families, giving up everything—not in the next life but in this life He will give you back houses, family, everything, and with them persecutions (see Mark 10:29-30). So there are rewards that you will receive; you get a return on everything. There is a one-hundredfold return. However, you will also get persecutions because there is a price to be paid for walking with God even after you are saved. Jesus said that if you seek the Kingdom and all its righteousness, all these things will come to you as well (see Matt. 6:33). It is all going to come to you and God is going to pay you back for everything that you have ever sacrificed for Him.

The teaching of the crucified life is supposed to be of great importance in these days that we are living in. It's not, but it should be. If you want to get something, you have to give it away; you have to give your life away to receive life. Jesus said if you try to preserve your life, you're going to lose it, but if you lose your life for His sake you gain it (see Matt. 16:25). That is the way the spirit realm works. Jesus is the One who said all these things because He wants you to prosper. However, He is asking for you to give so that it will be given back to you.

Give, and it will be given to you: good measure, pressed down, shaken together, and running over will be put into

*your bosom. For with the same measure that you use, it
will be measured back to you* (Luke 6:38).

God asks you to sow, and then you reap. He asks you to believe
first, and then you will receive. He said that when you pray and
stand, pray and believe, you receive what you're asking for and it shall
be yours (see Mark 11:24).

You see, it seems opposite to what the world says. The world says,
"I'll believe it when I see it." However, God says that you see it in
the spirit, but you do not see it the physical; you see it by faith. You
believe, then you see it by faith, and then you receive it. It is a spiritual thing. I see things in the spirit that I am going to receive, and I
do not see it with my physical eyes. It is not in my actual possession
yet, but I have the reality in my spirit; I see it. That is the faith that
believes that you receive it before you have it; the kind of faith that
moves mountains. It is the kind of faith that the people in the book
of Hebrews commended people for because they "saw Him who was
invisible" (see Heb. 11:27). You see the answer by faith in the Spirit.
God is asking you to look into the Spirit realm first and not in the
natural. The natural realm is not the real realm.

When you ask for something, you should always believe that you
will receive, and you will have it. Do not say what the world says.
"Well, when I see it, I will believe it," because that is not the way that
God created the whole universe. He purposed in His heart what He
wanted. He saw it in His heart, and then He spoke it out and then it
came into being. The manifestation was the final part of it.

ENCOUNTERING YOUR FUTURE

What is it that you need from God? What is it that is happening?
Do you feel stuck? Whatever it is you are going through right now,

you have to acknowledge that God is with you no matter where you are, according to Scripture, and recognize that He is guiding you and laying His hand upon you. God Almighty is lighting your path. He is igniting you inside with resurrection power from the Holy Spirit. He is strengthening you, and He is causing you to triumph over your enemies. He is causing you to know what turn to take when just a moment ago you did not know. And now, all of a sudden, you see it and you know what happened. You encountered your future because you encountered God. Jesus Christ is standing in your future, and so it is all rigged in your favor. Once you encounter Jesus, it shifts your reality and all of a sudden you know what to do next. You know what to say. You know how it is going to go. That is the way every Christian should operate. That is what I saw in Heaven, and that is why I came back. I want to teach people how to walk in the reality of Heaven right now and to get whatever it is that they need or want by believing God and then receiving it, not the other way around.

I am going to pray for you and impart to you from Heaven right now:

> *Father, in the name of Jesus, thank You for putting Your hand on the people right now. For each person reading this, in the name of Jesus, I thank You that Your Holy Spirit is guiding them and strengthening them. Nothing is going to be impossible if they will believe. Thank You! In Jesus' name, amen.*

Chapter 7

The I AM Is with You

*It's impossible to disappear from you or to
ask the darkness to hide me, for your presence
is everywhere, bringing light into my night.
There is no such thing as darkness with you.
The night, to you, is as bright as the day;
there's no difference between the two.*

—Psalm 139:11-12 TPT

I was shown the truth concerning Jesus being known as the great I AM. In an encounter with Jesus, I was shown the throne room and saw that the Trinity existed and met in order to plan the creation of our known universe before time was instituted on planet Earth. Each one of us was thought of by God in the timeless realm that the Trinity lives in continually.

When the heavenly Father thought of each individual person, He then had a personal book written about them and breathed their spirit out and sent them to their mother's womb. I saw that it is a person's free will to choose not to serve God and not follow what was written about them in Heaven. I saw that every person was also sent an angel to expedite and implement what was written about them if the person were to cooperate with God's perfect will.

I saw that to the degree to which the individual person operated through faith and obedience, according to what was given to them by God, that was how much they were rewarded and experienced the perfect will of God. Every person is given the ability to fulfill the perfect will of God through the Holy Spirit, the Word of God, and the angels. There is more than enough help for an individual to be a partaker of the divine nature through the promises that God has given to every man (see 2 Pet. 1:1-4).

I was given the understanding that we are judged by what was written by God beforehand, with all of the abilities that were given to us as gifts, and not by what we do in our own endeavors. When we stand before God, we have to give an account for what we did with what we were given. There are no rewards for disobedience or selfish endeavors. That is why it is so important as a Christian to know the will of God and to do it with all of your heart. I stood in the very place that I was created and gave an account of my life before Jesus. I saw that I was only operating in about 35 percent of what I could have. I immediately realized that I was not in full obedience or operating in the understanding of the true ways of my Father, God. It was a very humbling time for me because I realized that it was my responsibility to know the will of God and to bring it to fulfillment.

In this encounter with Jesus, it was clear to me that the very spot where God thought of me and breathed my spirit out into my mother's womb was also the spot where I stood before Him and was judged for what I had done in the flesh. I was standing before the great I AM. In this timeless realm that I stood in with Jesus, I saw that where I began is where I ended up. I gave an account to God of my earthly life, and no time had elapsed. God is not bound by time and distance like we are on this earth, and He wants to help us to fulfill His perfect will.

I AM Is with You

The power of God is ministering to people about the idea that our God, the I AM, is with us. God Himself is known as the I AM, and Jesus even referred to I AM in His ministry. I am going to share with you what it means to be associated with someone who is in the center of the universe and center of creation—the center of everything that is in existence. God is the origin of everything we see because He created everything. Psalm 139:11-12 is a divine passage of Scripture, and I am excited about this revelation that comes from the Word of God.

You will have to make adjustments within yourself to receive from the Lord in a new way. Many times we think we understand something, especially the Word of God, and then find out that we have been taught wrong or that we misinterpreted what was said. What I have found about Jesus is that it is just as important to understand the intent of what God is saying as it is to hear the actual words He has spoken. If God's purposes are not known, then we do not know His personality. People who love God want to know His heart, and I have found that God has a passionate heart.

God is very intentional every time Jesus speaks or appears to someone, and He has a purpose for all of the things that are being done on the earth through the Spirit of God. It is all in the intention of God, the planning of God, and His foreknowledge. We do not know everything about God. We can read about Him and we can experience Him, but we do not know God as we should. When I met Jesus, I realized this so clearly. I realized that I did not have the understanding that I needed, and I did not want to come back because I realized it was going to take a long time to get to know Jesus as intimately as I should.

Can you imagine? I am in Heaven, I am not in my body anymore, and I do not have the limitations that I had before. Now, all of a sudden, I realize that I am going to need at least the first thousand years of the millennial reign to get to know Jesus more intimately! Why? Because there is so much to have and there is so much to know about God the Father and Jesus the Son and the Holy Spirit. There is just no way to get to know Him as intimately as we think. I know that is hard to understand, and even in the time that I spent with Him, I got to know Him better. However, there are still so many questions that I had about His personality. The Holy Spirit wants to impart to us in this chapter about that very thing. I gathered some things about Jesus and His personality by spending time with Him, and I found out that He has a revelation of what it is like to be pre-existing. What I mean by that is that before the world was formed, I AM was there. In John 17, Jesus prayed that you would see and know what He knows. He said that the same love that the Father has for Him He has for you and that you would experience it and have the revelation of the glory that Jesus shared with the Father.

These things were in existence even while He was walking on the earth. He was pre-existent. He experienced the Father and was at the right hand of God. Then He came into Mary's womb and then through Mary and Joseph He grew up and walked this earth as a Son of God. He was given a body, but He did not originate from this realm. He originated from Heaven and was pre-existent. I AM means that He is the center of all existence; it is the center of understanding to have the revelation that God Himself is with you because He loves you.

God has the ability to do anything. There is no limitation; anything that you ask Him does not take Him by surprise and you cannot shut Him down, and you cannot break Him. He is going to have more than enough. He is the God who is the I AM. The psalmist is saying in Psalm 139:11 that it is impossible for anyone to disappear from God. You know you cannot hide from Him. You cannot have darkness hide you. To God, there is no darkness; you have to understand that He can see everything. God is full of light, and you cannot hide from Him.

He created man to be on this earth and to rule and reign with Him. When man fell, God lost His family; He lost His creation to the devil. The light of God is so bright in Heaven that you do not need the sun. There was no sun when I was in Heaven. It was the light of God; it illuminates all of Heaven. God does not have any darkness within Himself, and He does not have any to give out. There is no evil in Heaven and there is no darkness. It is a beautiful place that is all light and there can never be darkness.

THE SPIRITUAL PARALLEL

Two things must happen here. There is physical darkness and there is physical light, and then there is spiritual darkness and spiritual light. However, I saw in Heaven that both the darkness and the light used to be together both spiritually and physically and that they are now separated because this whole world fell. When this world fell, and we fell, then we could still see the physical part of it, but it was not that way before. There is a parallel in the spirit that looks just like this and the spirit realm is the real realm. Thus, the actual light of God is not physical light. It is the light of Heaven, which is spiritual; it is so bright and has substance to it. Everything in Heaven has substance to it. To God, the difference between the two is indistinguishable. In Psalm 139:11-12, it says that even darkness is light to God because He sees through everything. It is all lit up to God and He does not have limitations.

What I want to focus on is the fact that when the Spirit of the Lord comes, He illuminates. He is like a spotlight that reveals things that you did not see just a moment ago. When the Holy Spirit comes, which is very important in this life, He is the Light who lights your path. You have a path that is lit up, and the Holy Spirit is the One who illuminates it. The Holy Spirit lights your path because He wants you to know things and to see things.

Even though we have physical eyes and physical ears, we should not just focus on the physical realm. It is not just about how much you see and hear on earth. It is about developing your spiritual eyesight and spiritual hearing so that you can see into the spirit realm—which is the real realm. It is here that the I AM lives. I AM is here in this realm even though you cannot see Him. He is in the spirit realm, which is parallel; it is just as real as this earthly realm. When God shows up by His Spirit, I AM is showing up in the spirit realm. You may not see Him with your physical eyes, but you can see Him in the spirit. The spirit realm will open up to you as you increase your exposure to the Word of God and the truth that is in the Word that comes by the Spirit of God. The Holy Spirit can take the truth and illuminate it to you; it is all about revelation. And God, in His great infinite power, made everything out of nothing.

> *By faith [that is, with an inherent trust and enduring confidence in the power, wisdom and goodness of God]*

we understand that the worlds (universe, ages) were framed and created [formed, put in order, and equipped for their intended purpose] by the word of God, so that what is seen was not made out of things which are visible (Hebrews 11:3 AMP).

This mystery of the pre-existent I AM is further revealed in Colossians:

For through the Son everything was created, both in the heavenly realm and on the earth, all that is seen and all that is unseen. Every seat of power, a realm of government, principality, and authority—it was all created through him and for his purpose! (Colossians 1:16 TPT)

If God comes to visit you, you must allow Him to be in your life through the Spirit of God in your spirit. The born-again experience is how this begins. Then, by walking in the fear of the Lord and feeding your spiritual life every day, the great I AM will begin to shift your reality because He gets closer to you.

You may be saying, "Well, you know I am born again. I am a Christian, and God is close." Yes, but your revelation of your relationship with God grows daily. You do not know somebody entirely in just a short amount of time. To know someone well, you have to learn by being around them. It is the same way with God. You have to let the Holy Spirit and the Word of God work on you. The closeness that you experience is due to the fact that you have opened yourself up to the spirit realm.

It is no longer just the physical realm. It is the spiritual realm that is opening up to you. You are responsible for feeding your spirit man with food from Heaven, which is the Word of God. The pages of God's Word have to come alive and go into your spirit and become the food that helps you grow. The Word of God is the absolute truth. This is what I do. I feed myself on smaller portions of the Word of God. I study certain subjects and get the Scriptures together, and then I study them to get an overall view of a particular topic with plenty of scriptural support. If I know that something is true, but I cannot find enough scriptural support for it, then I just let it go. I focus on those things that I know have plenty of scriptural support. When we do that, we grow leaps and bounds. I start to participate in the supernatural every day, and I know that is what you also want. I am trying to teach you how to do things in the simplest way. There is a spirit realm, so you need to feed yourself from that realm, but you also must sow into that realm. It takes discipline to make your body and your mind align with your spirit. Because you are a spirit first, that part of you wants to participate in the supernatural. Your spirit man knows that it is "rigged in your favor," but your mind will try to logically reason out these truths. Your soul, which is your mind, will, and emotions, will try to talk you out of the supernatural and then your body cannot participate in it either.

Your body wants to talk you out of any spiritual activity and will act up by seeking attention. You may have your mind and your body acting up when there is a spiritual experience about to happen. For example, every time you pick your Bible up to read it or you start to pray in the spirit, asking God for help, you may encounter resistance. If there is resistance, a spiritual encounter is coming your way.

HEAVENLY SEASONS AND CYCLES

If you have revelation of the Word of God, you will have an encounter or a visitation where God visits you by His Spirit or by Jesus appearing or even by angelic visitation. First you receive revelation, and then visitation, which leads to habitation. And habitation is where God stays, and it is constant. It is habitation when it is no longer a visit, but rather it is continual. That is the way it should be for every Christian, but unfortunately it is not that way for many reasons.

One reason is that we do not discern that God is the great I AM. He is the center of everything, which means that it all started with Him and it will all end with Him. This truth is not the thought process that we have in this culture. If you look at the way we think, it's based in Greek thought. Greek culture has influenced us. We have a timeline, which is the way the Greeks thought. In other words, in history, the Greeks had hash marks or reference points to record history. You have a calendar and you chart out different events. There are holidays and other reference points. There is a 24-hour day and 365 days for a year. Greek thought differs from God's way and from the Hebraic way of thinking, which is all seasonal and cyclical.

In the spirit realm, I saw that the point where something started was also where it finished. When God was sitting on His throne, He thought of you and He breathed you into your mother's womb. Then you became a living soul, and your body was formed in the womb. You were born, you grew up, and then at the end of your life you will pass away.

What happens is that your spirit returns to the place where you were born, the place where you were first thought of by God. Ultimately, you stand before God and give an account for your life, and that is the way it is. You give an account and then God determines where you go for all eternity. It is incredible to me how we do not have this kind of thinking. It is a shock to many people when they get to Heaven because they did not understand the ways of God.

God, in the I AM realm, is the one who starts everything and then He is the one who finishes everything. He does not even have to get off His throne because you come to Him. You were breathed out of Him into your mother's womb and you come back around. At the end of your life, you appear before Him and He has not even had to get off His throne. He does not even have to stand up because everything starts with God and everything ends with God. This is important because when light goes out from God, it comes back to Him. When God sends out His Word, it always comes back with the desired result.

> *So shall My word be that goes forth out of My mouth: it shall not return to Me void [without producing any effect, useless], but it shall accomplish that which I please and purpose, and it shall prosper in the thing for which I sent it* (Isaiah 55:11 AMPC).

God is not bound by anything except His Word. He loves humanity and the heavenly Father expressed that love by sending Jesus as the ultimate sacrifice. He decides something in His heart and then He speaks it, which in turn becomes law. What God has done is spoken you into existence and wrote a book about you. He sends you into your mother's womb and waits for His Word to be performed. He has written about your life in a book in Heaven and that book is looked at by the angels who come down and enforce it (see Ps. 139:16).

You can choose to enjoy this life, or you can dread and hate it—it's up to you. You can choose blessings, or you can choose curses. You have to decide which one you are going to do. You can yield to joy and be obedient to what God has spoken to you. You can seek God and find out that He is the great I AM. Alternatively, you can ignore your spiritual life, make bad decisions, and you do your own thing. Either way, at the end of your life you are going to have to give an account of what you did with what you were given.

DISCERNING GOD'S GIFTS

It is incredible to me that when I was with Jesus, I saw that I received so much that I had not discerned previously. I discovered that I had not done what I should have with what He had given me even though I had rewards and I was going to Heaven, and even though Jesus congratulated me and told me that I had been faithful. I saw that God had given me a gift and I did not appreciate it, and I did not discern it. So, I am back again, talking to you because God has shown me that He does not have the limitations we have. If you ask Him, He is going to show you favor and He is going to perform miracles for you. You can live this life out victoriously!

You must remember that darkness to God is as light. Rules do not bind Him, and He is not bound by darkness. Psalm 139:11-12 is talking about the fact that that there is no darkness with Him. If it is dark down here on the earth and if you are going through a dark period of your life to where you are struggling, God is not worried. He is not going to leave you. He is going to enter your life, and when He comes there is going to be a bright light. There is going to be light shining into the darkness. There is going to be light that expels the darkness. It is going to happen in your life as you begin to listen to what I am saying, as there is a transfer of the impartation to you that I received from Heaven.

When God comes to you and visits you, and when you read the Word of God, it illuminates your path. The psalmist said, "Thy word is a lamp under my feet and a light to my path" (see Ps. 119:105). That is what we encounter when we seek God. I know you need help, because everyone needs help. Everyone wants to know what God has for them. If you are a Christian, it is natural that you want to know what God is saying and what He has planned for you.

The most important thing is hearing God's voice. He is not soft-spoken; His voice is loud and clear. You may be encountering warfare and other demonic voices that are more evident to you. It is not that God is quiet, it is just that you have to shut out all the voices of the world. You have to set yourself apart, and that's when you will start to hear from God. You have to fine-tune yourself by studying, meditating, and partaking of the Word of God and by letting it get into your spirit. The Word is like bread from Heaven. When you eat of the Word, it builds you up, encourages you, and causes you to be a spiritual giant. And that is what is going to happen. You grow to the point where the devil cannot handle you anymore and the demons will leave you alone. They will get to the place where it is counterproductive for them to waste their time with you because you know who you are. You are a child of God and He is the great I AM. He is the finisher of your faith, not just the starter.

Humble yourself and realize that God is speaking loudly. It is the fact that you have so many other voices in your life that you need to start tuning out and focus on the voice of God alone. I will tell you what it sounds like—it sounds like the Word of God and it feels like the Spirit of God. There is a spiritual sense of fire and power in the Spirit of God. That is how the Word of God also feels; when you read it, it's fire. You can also hear God's voice in the Word of God because it is the framework of what God has already said.

When the fire of the Spirit and the Word of God mix, you hear God's voice, and it is more precise. When God speaks to you, He is going to speak to you in a familiar way just as the Scriptures are written. When the presence of God comes into your life, you sense Him spiritually and you feel the fire, and there is encouragement. When you sense His presence and His fire, you will know that you are on the right track.

I feel the fire and I know that God is with me and that He is in what I am doing. The Word of God is useful for teaching and doctrine to develop your faith in believing the right things. The Word will correct the wrong ideas and it will give strength in those things which are true. When God comes in and begins to shift your world—because He is the great I AM—you start to realize that God is the central figure in your life and you recognize that there is no appeal beyond Him. Whatever you need in this life, you can go to Him and know that He is the ultimate authority. There is no one else you can appeal to; I AM is your final appeal. You can go to the Father in Jesus' name and say, "Father, this is what I want."

There are demon spirits that want your attention and they will rile up the flesh and cause your body to want attention. They will rile up your soul so that your mind, your will, and your emotions go haywire. There will be all kinds of drama in your life, and the whole time it's demons instigating it through the flesh and your soul. Your spirit is connected to God's Spirit, the great I AM. There is a stability in your heart and in your spirit that will cause you to "know that you know" your position in God.

You will know your position in God and be encouraged in your spirit. However, you must tell your soul what it believes. You have to tell your body what it is going to do. It will not just do it on its own. Your mind will not think the right thoughts on its own. If it is left to its own, it will go toward the way that it wants to go, which is usually the wrong way. To educate your soul by discipline, you teach your body by training it not to go astray. You say, "We are not going to do this," and then you tell your soul, "We are not going to think this; we are not going to feel this."

Encourage yourself in the Lord and know that God has written individual plans for you in advance. God has no problems with accomplishing miracles. There is a miracle flow coming from Heaven right now and God is moving by His Spirit in your life. You need to receive, right now, in the name of Jesus.

Chapter 8

THE LORD CREATED YOU

*You formed my innermost being, shaping my
delicate inside and my intricate outside, and
wove them all together in my mother's womb. I
thank you, God, for making me so mysteriously
complex! Everything you do is marvelously
breathtaking. It simply amazes me to think
about it! How thoroughly you know me, Lord.*

—PSALM 139:13-14 TPT

EVERY GENERATION HAS A PURPOSE THAT GOD HAS
designed for the advancement of His Kingdom.
Additionally, every individual in each generation has an
important part to play in God's plan. I was shown by the
Lord Jesus how important it is to speak by the Spirit of God
to a generation if you are called to do so. Throughout history, most people within a generation do not discern their
need for their purpose. When prophets speak by the Spirit

of God to a generation, they are usually considered to be out of order and are often silenced for speaking the truth. However, the next generation celebrates the prophets as heroes because they were correct in what they spoke to the previous generation. As the Lord Jesus showed me this truth, He encouraged me to speak to this generation of believers so that the next generation will not have to write or speak about how we missed *our day of visitation.*

I saw that most people today do not discern their need for God's help. Prophets often call out for people to repent and humble themselves for God to show a generation what they are missing. In the book of Revelation, Jesus shared with John His concern for the seven churches. Jesus said many times that the truth is hidden so that only certain individuals have eyes that see and ears that hear. Because of this, Jesus told me to always pray that the eyes of my heart would be enlightened and flooded with revelation, according to what the apostle Paul spoke of in Ephesians. *"I pray that your hearts will be flooded with light so that you can understand the confident hope he has given to those he called—his holy people who are his rich and glorious inheritance"* (Eph. 1:18 NLT).

I am going to discuss some of what I was shown, when I was with Jesus in the heavenly realms, about God's role in planning your life before you were born. God created you in your mother's womb. It is all set up for you to win. It is not just a pep talk, and it is not just positive speech. It is the way God set things up because He is that way.

He does not think He is going to fail. I have never met an angel that thought that they were going to fail at what they were assigned to do either. Failure cannot be found in Heaven; it is not the culture of Heaven to lose or fail. We do not plan on failing because God does not fail.

God does not try things out; rather, He is a Person who succeeds. He plans things out and He does not speak unless He means it. Jesus is very conscientious about what He says, so He does not jokingly say things because He will get everything He says. He thinks it out because He wants to speak out what He will receive. That is the way He wants to teach us. That is why He told His disciples in Mark 11:23-24 that if you have a mountain, you can speak to it. If you believe in your heart that what you say with your mouth shall come to pass, you shall have it.

This is the way it was set up when we were created in the image of God as expressed in Genesis 1:16. We were created that way because we were like God. It was amazing to me when I was in Heaven how much more we are like God than anyone would want to teach down here. It becomes very controversial when you see what we should be and realize how fallen we have been.

While we are on the earth, we do not realize this truth. But when we are in Heaven, we lose our body and we get another body, mind, will, and emotions that are redeemed. Down here, we have to deal with everything about us that needs to be transformed, but in Heaven it is already changed. When I was there, I did not have the resistance that I have down here. There was no battle, and I was able to discern what God wanted and act on it without resistance.

MYSTERIOUSLY COMPLEX

In Heaven, I saw that the way that God created me from the beginning was to be like Him. Adam and Eve were like God in the Garden and that is why God liked to come down and talk with them. He would physically walk and talk with them. Now that we live in a fallen world, we cannot even see into the spirit realm unless the Holy

Spirit opens our eyes. Angels could be all around you right now, but you would not even know it because you cannot see it. However, if you learn to develop your spiritual life and learn to develop sensitivity to the things of God in the spirit realm, then you can start to discern and know that there are angels around you and that many things are going on all the time around you. Be encouraged; the Lord has created you.

> *You formed my innermost being, shaping my delicate inside and my intricate outside, and wove them all together in my mother's womb. I thank you, God, for making me so mysteriously complex! Everything you do is marvelously breathtaking. It simply amazes me to think about it! How thoroughly you know me, Lord! You even formed every bone in my body when you created me in the secret place, carefully, skillfully shaping me from nothing to something* (Psalm 139:13-15 TPT).

Think about the fact that God is perfect and that He does not come from an imperfect world like the one we have become accustomed to. Many people down here do not understand perfection. They do not understand anything about the ways of God because there is no way to comprehend while in an imperfect environment.

In this realm, everything is slow, but in Heaven it is fast. When you say something, you get it. When you think something, then you see it. In Heaven, there are no restrictions. You can talk without even moving your lips. You can go to places simply by thinking. You do not have to get on a plane and travel for hours. Everything about Heaven is simplified. This fallen world is not able to understand God because He is not like this fallen world. This fallen world is not His fault.

The psalmist noted that it is "mysteriously complex," that every-thing the Lord does is marvelous and breathtaking. That is the God I met, and that is the Heaven I experienced. It is up to us how much of God we encounter down here. You can have supernatural events every day if you want them. If you want to encounter God in an inti-mate way, you must make your move toward Him. You will begin to walk with Him just like He did with Adam and Eve in the Garden (see Gen. 3:8).

You have to start feeling comfortable with God. But how do you feel comfortable with God when He is so holy, awesome, all-pow-erful, and fearsome? How do you feel comfortable with that? God created you in His image, and He created you in a way to commu-nicate with Him. In the Garden of Eden, God communicated with Adam and Eve face to face. Now God communicates through His Son, Jesus, and by the Holy Spirit.

Jesus speaks the things that He has done by the blood. You are forgiven because of Jesus' blood, and the Holy Spirit testifies about this. Jesus is speaking, and the Holy Spirit testifies through you. The Holy Spirit continually wants to pray through you and guide you. He wants to be an advocate and support. He is the one who is going to cause you to triumph in every challenge that you have ever expe-rienced on this earth. The Holy Spirit is in you. Jesus speaks to the Father and says, "This person is forgiven because I shed my blood for him." The Father, in turn, forgives you based on the testimony of Jesus.

All of this activity is happening around you all the time, but it is all hidden because we do not have any concept of it in the fallen world. You cannot conceive of how perfect God is because you have never encountered it, but God is perfect no matter what you think or feel. He is completely perfect, and when He formed you He did not make an accident. He did not make a mistake; He made you with intention.

SPEAKING WITH INTENTION

We have talked about this before, but it is important to note God's intention and what He says. If you hear someone speaking, you can understand the intention of why that was said, and it opens up revelation to you. What are people saying when they speak, and what is going on behind the scenes? The Spirit of the Lord is speaking, and He has intention. He is thinking about your future, thinking about what God has planned for you. He speaks with the intention to guide you; He has an insight that you do not have. God made you mysteriously complex because you are a spirit being that is in a body, which is your "earth-suit." You have a soul, which is your mind, will, and emotions, and you have your body. These parts of you do not always cooperate with God, and they do not cooperate with your spirit.

God could be doing many things in your spirit, and you could be listening and doing what God is saying, but your body and your soul (again, that's your mind, will, and emotions) could be fighting you the whole time. It is amazing to think that you actually oppose yourself! We are separated into three parts, and two of those parts are not redeemed. When you were born again, your spirit was recreated, and you became a new creature in Christ. The old has passed and new has come (see 2 Cor. 5:17); however, your mind was not. Romans 12:2 explains that your mind must be renewed, and it has to be transformed by the renewing of the mind.

Your mind has to be renewed by the Word of God. You have to condition your mind to think the way that you are supposed to. It is not going to do it on its own. Paul said, "Listen! After I preach Christ, if I do not discipline myself, if I do not discipline my body, it will cause me to be disqualified from the race and lose out" (see 1 Cor. 9:27).

Paul was an apostle who preached everywhere. However, he said that if he allowed his body to rule him and yielded to what it wanted, then it would disqualify him. That is amazing to me because Paul was led by the Spirit, yet he could have been disqualified. You cannot allow every thought that you think to be the truth, because you have to measure it up with the truth that is in the Word of God. When people say something that is wrong (and it does not matter who they are), you must measure it according to Scripture. Find out what the Bible says about it.

When I was in Heaven, Jesus was not asking my opinion. He never asked me what I thought. He told me what the truth was. He was continually telling me that this is the way it is. Jesus would quote Scripture to me continually. When I came back, I had a different way of looking at things because I saw that it is not up to what I think; it is what I know is the truth.

When God speaks, it is the absolute truth. He framed the world with His words. When He created man in His image, that is exactly what He did. We must watch our words, just like God has to watch His words, because when He speaks it goes out and comes back around and accomplishes that which He intended according to Isaiah 55:11. Jesus said to watch your words because you will be judged by them.

> *But I say to you that for every idle word men may speak, they will give account of it in the day of judgment* (Matthew 12:36).

Words are critical. Jesus explained to me that this is because the Father created human beings in His likeness. We must be careful because we are saying things and not realizing that we are commanding the atmosphere around us. In other words, when you say something, you're giving out a command. Jesus showed me that because people are not watchful over their words, their words become diluted. It causes them to be ineffective because they say all kinds of things that they do not mean. Then when they actually say something, it no longer takes effect. Be careful that you stay sharp and that you walk with God in the Spirit. It involves recognizing that when God formed you He made you mysteriously complex. He knows you because He made you and formed you in your mother's womb. The psalmist said that He created you in the secret place.

THE MYSTERY OF THE SECRET PLACE

There is a great deal of mystery to the secret place. When you are there, you get ahold of mysteries that have been hidden. God will speak to you, but it is in a whisper. That is also where you were created—in the secret place. God created you in the secret place, carefully and skillfully shaping you from nothing into something. Do you know how hard it is for us to take nothing and make something out of it? We breeze over some of these things and do not consider how difficult it is to make something out of nothing, but God can do it! He can take something that does not exist, imagine it, speak it, and then it comes into existence. He can create things by His words.

When God made man in His image, He gave us the ability, through prayer and proclamation, to speak out and guide our life. We cause things to happen by our command; we have been given authority. Jesus' name is mighty, and we should not take it in vain. We should not say it when we do not mean it. That is what it means to take the Lord's name in vain. When you invoke the name of God, all of Heaven and all creation stand still. When you say the name of

Jesus Christ, you are proclaiming the Head of the universe, and it is a very powerful thing to say. When you say His name in vain, you are not recognizing His authority. You do not recognize how powerful that name is.

After you were created, you became a living soul who was born, and you began to breathe. You were spiritual, and you were physically in your mother's womb, but then you came out of your mother's womb and you became physical. You became a living being who walks this earth now. When this occurred, you grew up in maturity.

The maturing process would have been helped if you were taught that your words are important and that you were made in the image of God. However, people do not teach these things. The world certainly is not going to give it to you and satan does not want you to walk in God's authority; he does not want you to walk in this revelation at all. It has been kept from you because satan wants to keep the church powerless. The truth of the matter is that it is impossible for the church to be powerless because Jesus said that the gates of hell will not prevail against it. The gates of hell cannot and will not prevail against the church of the living God.

That is the truth. However, people must be made aware that they need to transform their mind. They need to start to get on God's side of everything. You come from this place where you are intricately and fearfully made, and now you develop, and you mature, and then you start to speak. There comes this time when you know that you know that you know what God has said to you. Out of this knowledge, you begin to believe and confess that manifestation is going to start to come in this realm because you are taking something that was born in your heart, through faith, and was made in the image of God. The same Spirit that raised Jesus from the dead is dwelling in you, and that same power is causing you to speak. When you speak, you better really know what you are saying because you have been given authority in this earth realm.

You are a spirit in a body that speaks, and you have all the power of Heaven that has been given to you in the name of Jesus. You have received the resurrection power of Jesus Christ, who is the Holy Spirit. He is inside of you. God the Father in Heaven says that if you ask anything in the name of Jesus, it will be given to you that your joy may be full (see John 16:24). Do you want your joy to be full? God wants your joy to be full and He wants you to see the manifestation in this life.

God skillfully shaped you from nothing to something, and now that you are something you are going somewhere to be somebody so that the manifestation of the sons of God can be revealed.

> *For the earnest expectation of the creation eagerly waits for the revealing of the sons of God. For the creation was subjected to futility, not willingly, but because of Him who subjected it in hope; because the creation itself also will be delivered from the bondage of corruption into the glorious liberty of the children of God* (Romans 8:19-21).

THE MILLENNIAL REIGN

When I was with Jesus and He was just a few feet from me during my 1992 visitation with Him, He told me that Christians on the earth should not simply be surviving, but that in actuality Christians are to be thriving. He told me that we are qualifying for our position in the millennial reign. What He said shocked me because He showed me all these things and He told me that I was on probation now for the next life, even though I was already going to Heaven.

You are not down here surviving. As a Christian you are down here learning and maturing and getting ready for your assignment. At that very moment, I realized why I was created.

I looked and I had this beautiful robe on. It was an ambassador's robe, and in the millennial reign I was assigned over territories and countries and given rank. I was in charge and I had angels under me. I saw that one day I will rule and reign with Him in the next life and that I was not down here surviving, I was down here qualifying.

Be encouraged and take this to heart. Everything you go through is working for your good because you love God and have been called according to His purpose (see Rom. 8:28). All things are going to work together for your good. *It is rigged in your favor* because God has written things about you and they must come to pass. If they do not, it is because you did not cooperate with Heaven. Angels come to help you cooperate. The Holy Spirit comes in full manifestation to help you, to be an Advocate and a Helper, to cause you to do the things that you could not do on your own. He causes you to be empowered.

Say yes to godliness and make the right decisions that will empower you to say no to ungodliness and no to the flesh. The Holy Spirit wants you to fulfill that which is written about you in Heaven—your destiny. It has to do with favor and with having an intimate walk with God. I know that you want that, but when I was in Heaven I saw that if we do not cooperate with what has been written about us then we do not get it.

God is waiting for us to say yes to Him, even if we do not know what it is. I have this habit, and you should too, where I tell God yes. This is my daily prayer, and I invite you to pray it with me:

> *Lord, whatever it is that You have for me, whatever it is that You desire for me, whatever is written about me in*

Heaven, I agree with it! Open my books, Lord, and put Your finger on what is for me today, and whatever it says about me I agree with You. Let it be implemented right now; Holy Spirit, implement it in my life. Empower me to do what has been written.

 **God Almighty created you so that you would trust Him with all things. Some want God to give them everything but are unwilling to give God everything.**

When you embrace the fact that *it's all rigged in your favor*, you will begin to see the impossible become possible in your life. What are you holding back from your loving heavenly Father? We know that God has everything, so what could He possibly want from us? Well, when I met Jesus, I realized that He needed our will. That is a profound truth because God will not force Himself on anyone. He wants those who truly love Him and want to reconcile with Him. The apostle Paul explained to us how we should live our lives from now on as Christians:

> *For I know that this will turn out for my deliverance through your prayer and the supply of the Spirit of Jesus Christ, according to my earnest expectation and hope that in nothing I shall be ashamed, but with all bold-ness, as always, so now also Christ will be magnified in*

*my body, whether by life or by death. **For to me, to live
is Christ, and to die is gain. But if I live on in the
flesh, this will mean fruit from my labor;** yet what I
shall choose I cannot tell. For I am hard-pressed between
the two, having a desire to depart and be with Christ,
which is far better. Nevertheless to remain in the flesh is
more needful for you. And being confident of this, I know
that I shall remain and continue with you all for your
progress and joy of faith, that your rejoicing for me may
be more abundant in Jesus Christ by my coming to you
again* (Philippians 1:19-26).

The apostle Paul had the mindset that if he was to continue
living, Christ Jesus could have his body in order to manifest the ministry that Jesus had when He was on the earth. He knew that if he
left, that would be good for him, but not good for those whom he
was ministering to as they would be left without him. So, we must
keep this mindset as well in our daily lives. We remain here in this
earthly realm so that Jesus can produce fruit through us. With heartfelt passion, we must give ourselves completely over to Jesus so that
He can live His life through us. *"Therefore, my beloved, as you have
always obeyed, not as in my presence only, but now much more in my
absence, work out your own salvation with fear and trembling; for it
is God who works in you both to will and to do for His good pleasure"*
(Phil. 2:12-13).

Your body, as a Christian, is no longer your own. Most in the
Body of Christ do not understand this truth. We were bought by the
blood of Jesus and entered into adoption through Jesus into the heavenly Father's family. The apostle Paul said, *"Or do you not know that
your body is the temple of the Holy Spirit who is in you, whom you have
from God, and you are not your own? For you were bought at a price;*

therefore glorify God in your body and in your spirit, which are God's" (1 Cor. 6:19-20).

When will we as believers enter into the revelation that we get everything that God has for us when we finally give Him everything that we have? We need to crucify the flesh and be set free to receive the supernatural. Truly, *it's rigged in your favor!* The apostle Paul received this revelation of giving God everything and announced to the Corinthian church, *"I affirm, by the boasting in you which I have in Christ Jesus our Lord, I die daily"* (1 Cor. 15:31).

INTIMACY WITH GOD

Interestingly, most people in the Old Testament did not understand their calling. They did not understand their life in general, and God would interrupt their life. He would talk to them. He would visit them. Sometimes He would send prophets, like Samuel, and He would anoint them as a king or as a prophet. It is fascinating that in the Old Testament, many times God had to interrupt people's lives with the supernatural to get them to do the right thing. When people did not do the right thing, then they had to face the consequences of that. King David, even though he was an excellent king, a worshiper, and a friend of God, still did things wrong, and he suffered for it.

In the New Testament, there was a profound change; people do not have this fear of the Lord in their life. People do not discern that He is the high and lofty one and that He also dwells with those who have a humble and contrite heart (see Ps. 51:17). Isaiah says this because God revealed Himself to Isaiah and he wrote that the Lord is high and lifted up and the train of His robe filled the temple (see Isa. 6:1). He spoke of what he saw in the throne room and how holy God is. He has not changed a bit. It surprises me that we see in the New

Testament how the Holy Spirit is given to guide and help us, and the Word of God is also given to guide us, and yet we do not even do as well as some of the people in the Old Testament.

What I see is missing, and what I want to start turning around and prevent from happening, is that many are not discerning who the Lord is or even discerning who *you* are. You must be able to accept God as He is. He is an awesome, holy God who does not need us. However, He wants us, and because He has chosen to pursue us we should let Him catch us. Once He catches us, we should allow Him to have fellowship with us.

We should look at God not just as our Creator, but as Someone who wants to sit, talk, and share with us. That is the God we read about in the Old Testament. When He asked Moses to come up the mountain and bring the people with him, the people would not come, and God was hurt. He was expecting all the people to celebrate that He had brought them out of Egypt. However, the children of Israel did not want any part of that intimacy.

Then when Jesus came, the disciples did not discern the intimacy. Jesus was puzzled by the fact that they were unbelieving and that they were not grasping the things that He was saying. It was because of their unbelief. John the disciple wrote that he was the one Jesus loved and was represented as being the closest of all the disciples. John is the only person out of the twelve who expressed this. Many of the people around Jesus did not want that level of intimacy with Him because of disbelief.

Paul persecuted the Christians until he met Jesus on the road to Damascus. When Jesus presented him with his persecution, he asked, "Who are You, Lord?" Or in other words, he was asking, "How did I persecute You, Lord?" Paul was thinking he was persecuting Christians, not God. Jesus explained to Paul that when he was persecuting Christians, he was directly persecuting Jesus. So, it hit Paul that God was sticking up for the believers who were called Christians. Paul was having Christians killed (see Acts 9).

We have come to a place where we have drawn away from intimacy. At the end of the age, we get to this place where we are just down here surviving and waiting for Jesus to come back. However, there are things that Jesus said must happen for Him to come back, and we are not doing those things—such as preaching the Gospel to the whole world. We are not going out into the harvest field like we should and bringing them in. China, Russia, and the Middle East must all enter into God's Kingdom. These people groups must come into the Kingdom, and then the end will happen. And yet, believers do not want to do the things that we know we should be doing.

In these last days, men's hearts are going to grow cold and people are going to call wrong right and right wrong. These days are upon us now. When I was in Heaven, I saw that God wants intimacy because He made us so intricately to have fellowship, face to face, with Him, and yet we are so resistant to that. The Holy Spirit and Jesus both want to have this intimacy. Be encouraged and let the Holy Spirit take you to that place right now. I believe that God is imparting this reality to you in Jesus' name.

Chapter 9

THE LORD HAS WRITTEN ABOUT YOU

You saw who you created me to be before I became me! Before I'd ever seen the light of day, the number of days you planned for me were already recorded in your book.

—Psalm 139:16 TPT

I KNOW THAT GOD HAS RIGGED EVERYTHING IN OUR favor, and I want to teach you how to engage God to the point where you start to see these things manifesting in your life. The devil seeks to slander God. You are going to get resistance after reading this because satan knows that if you hear and believe what you are reading, you are going to break free of his bondage. This happens all the time. I had to go through it, and you are going to have to go through it.

The Word of God is strong and active like a two-edged sword, and it divides between the soul and the Spirit (see

Heb. 4:12). God's Word will show you what your soul (your mind, will, and emotions) is saying, and will also show you what your spirit is saying, which is the place where God's Spirit is dwelling. The Word of God actively divides between the soul and the spirit. So be encouraged when things come against you, because satan is trying to keep you in a small place. In fact, at this moment, satan knows that what you are reading is producing faith, and when faith is produced, the manifestation, or the action produced by faith, is coming. When that manifestation comes, not only is satan going to lose his hold on you, but he is going to lose his grip on everyone around you. You are going to manifest God's glory, and he knows that if he can slow you down or stop you then he can prevent other people from moving in this as well. We are going to be consistent. We are going to be diligent, and we are going to actively wield the Sword of the Spirit wherever we go.

Psalm 139:16 says, *"You saw who you created me to be before I became me!"* (TPT). God is saying that He had already seen you before He even created you and before you ever saw the light of day. *"Before I'd ever seen the light of day, the number of days you planned for me were already recorded in your book."* God's plan for you is profound and can be difficult to comprehend.

The reason that I have written this book is to help you get to this place quickly because you do not have to prolong this journey. You can just read these verses in your Bible and accept them. When you do, your spirit ignites in power and becomes so bright that even angels will gasp when they see the power of the resurrection in your spirit. My wife and I have seen and heard angels gasp. When we got hit by God, He ignited our very being with the glory of God, and angels were affected all around us as a result.

When the glory of God hits you and ignites your spirit, what happens is that you start to be who you are. That is what this verse in

Psalms is talking about. Lord, you created me before I became me. You already saw me, and You already knew me. Your heavenly Father is saying, "I remember the day I thought of you and I breathed you into your mother's womb, and you turned out just fine. You turned out just like I had thought of you."

CREATED TO SUCCEED

When Jesus showed this verse to me, I realized at that very moment that even though I did not understand the truth or even know the verse at the time, it was still valid. Jesus had to teach me this verse, and I had to find it in the Bible. He told me He thought of me in eternity past, and that He formed me in His mind first, and then sent me into my mother's womb. He breathed my spirit into my body in the womb, and I became a living soul. When I was born, I was created to succeed in everything that God had written about me. There was not a day that was written for me that was meant to fail, and it was a fantastic thing to see. Jesus showed me that it was this fallen world that was working against me from day one.

God never makes mistakes, so we are not mistakes. God intended for us to walk in authority on this earth. There is a fallen world with physical defects that happen because of genetics, because mankind has done wrong in this realm. We have abused our bodies, and then that transfers down to following generations. There are certain things in our diet, as well as chemicals and elements in our environment, that cause mutations in our genes. I am talking about God's intention for your life and that He did not do these bad things to you. You were born in a fallen world, and there are certain limitations in this fallen world, but your spirit man is perfect in the sight of God because He created you.

You got to a certain age, and you decided to do wrong. Paul said "sin revived and I died" (see Rom. 7:9). In other words, you have a sin problem in your life. You were born in this sin, and as a Christian you repented of your sins and turned away from them. You have asked Jesus to come into your heart, and when you did that you were accepting Him as your Savior—as the Person who took your place and was punished on your behalf. Jesus replaced you and took your punishment upon Himself so that you would not suffer punishment, and thus you don't go to hell because He went there for you. He suffered, died, and went to the belly of the earth. Jesus was risen from the dead, rose to the right hand of God, and is seated there right now.

He redeemed you in power, and because He created you He wants you to thank Him and live for Him. He wants you to live out His intentions for you—the intentions that have been written in your book. However, if people do not accept Him, they are not redeemed. They do not have the power to live out the book that was written about them, so they do not fulfill even one day of what has been written in their books in Heaven. I saw that people go to hell and they should not have because it was not written in their book to be there.

Their book did not come to pass because they did not engage God. They did not accept Jesus as their Savior, so they had to pay for their sins themselves. Jesus has already paid. It is like if you were standing in line to get into an event, and the person in front of you paid for your ticket, but you wanted to pay for your own, and so you double pay. Jesus already paid for your sins. He suffered and died for all humanity, and yet people will not accept Him. They will not take that gift, and the result is that the price is too high and people are unable to pay for it themselves. They end up going to hell and that is how they pay for it. They are punished for their sins because they did not accept that Jesus is Lord of their life.

God planned your days. He planned on you coming to Heaven. Jesus has discussed this with me at length. He wanted everyone to go to Heaven, so Jesus and the Father planned out everyone's book as though they would be redeemed and come to be with Him forever. Then Jesus came to earth and preached and led people to God the Father. Jesus died for us and rose from the dead before taking His seat at the right hand of God.

Unsaved people must accept what God has done or they do not get to go to Heaven. People will go through their whole life and not accept Jesus as Lord. When He came to earth, He had purposed to come and buy back humanity for the Father, and all these things are written in a book. Jesus said, "Everyone is supposed to come to Heaven. I bought everyone back, but if they do not acknowledge Me as Savior, they do not get in." It was heartbreaking when Jesus told me all the things that He did for people to help them and to redeem them. His voice was sad when He talked about how they will not accept Him or acknowledge what He did for them.

HEAVENLY REALMS

I want to encourage you, as a Christian, to walk in in the Spirit of God. You have to walk in power. You have to walk in demonstration of the Gospel and not in belief only, because what Jesus bought for us was much greater than what we know. Jesus, at length, explained to me the different things that He had accomplished for us. These things were hidden except through the writings of Paul the apostle, who was caught up into Heaven and saw these things, and what he could talk about, he did.

Paul's letters to the early churches make up a great deal of the New Testament. In them, Paul was writing about the spirit realm and about our position in the spirit realm. Jesus placed us back in the heart of the Father and seated us with Him in the heavenly realms at the right hand of God.

In the book of Revelation, the beginning two chapters are addressing the seven churches. It says that if you overcome and are victorious, you will sit with Jesus on a throne.

> *He raised us up with Christ the exalted One, and we ascended with him into the glorious perfection and authority of the heavenly realm, for we are now co-seated as one with Christ!* (Ephesians 2:6 TPT)

We are partakers of the divine nature according to Second Peter 1:4 where God, through Jesus Christ, has redeemed us and placed the Spirit of God inside of us so that we can walk in this reality. God thoroughly knows and understands you; it is a fantastic thing to think about, and He has written every day of your life in a book. It amazes me that people would not want to focus on that more.

SPEAKING OUT MYSTERIES

One of the ways to place more focus on God's written book for you is to allow the Holy Spirit to pray through you. You can begin to quote your book from Heaven. You can confirm, in the spirit, by speaking forth the mysteries that are in your book. By doing this, you actually quote God's perfect will!

> *Likewise the Spirit also helps in our weaknesses. For we do not know what we should pray for as we ought, but the Spirit Himself makes intercession for us with groanings which cannot be uttered* (Romans 8:26).

The Holy Spirit is going to help you to pray out perfect prayers as you connect your spirit with the Holy Spirit—in your weakness, not in your strength. God is going to strengthen you in your weakness and you are going to become strong. Paul actually gloried in his weaknesses. He said when you are weak, then you are made strong because God's strength is revealed in your weakness and then God comes in by His power. Romans 8:26 teaches that the Spirit comes into our weakness and helps us to pray prayers that we could not have articulated. The Holy Spirit causes us to pray perfect prayers.

I saw that what is written about us can be spoken by praying in the Spirit. When we pray in the Spirit, we are confirming it to all of Heaven, all of the angels, and all of hell. Everyone is hearing us speak out, by the Spirit, God's perfect will for our lives. It would be best if you yielded to the Holy Spirit as much as possible. You need to speak by the Spirit and allow the Holy Spirit to cause you to triumph in every circumstance.

When you come to realize how special you are, you will understand that God has *rigged it all in your favor*. You will begin to sense a separation between you and the world that you live in. You will begin to see that the world is not treating you as they should. The world does not deserve a Christian. In a fallen state, the world rejects Christianity and rejects Jesus Christ. The world killed Jesus, and they are going to want to kill you; they are going to want to stop the message that Jesus preached.

If you are going to preach the message of the Gospel, then you are going to encounter resistance. There is a setting apart that happens and it is because the Holy Spirit is holy. He wants to set you apart so that you are separate from what is unclean.

> *What friendship does God's temple have with demons?*
> *For indeed, we are the temple of the living God, just*
> *as God has said: I will make my home in them and*

walk among them. I will be their God, and they will be my people. For this reason, "Come out from among them and be separate," says the Lord. "Touch nothing that is unclean, and I will embrace you" (2 Corinthians 6:16-17 TPT).

You are holy, and the Lord has put His name on you. He owns you—you are His private stock, and He wants you for Himself. The Almighty God is going to display you to the world. Because He owns you, the world cannot touch you; they can only behold you. At the end of this age, we will start to see that there are things written about us. As you come into this revelation, the shift is going to happen. You will realize you are a lot more special than you and the people around you have discerned.

People are not going to treat you correctly if they do not discern who you are. They are going to think you are just a common man when in reality you are a son or daughter of God. You have been bought with a price and given a position. God owns you and you are more important than the spirit of this world and the people who have chosen to be in rebellion. You are more favored by God than they are, because they are resisting, and in turn God resists the proud.

God's going to resist them, but He is going to give grace to the humble. If you stay humble and you set yourself apart, then what will happen is that God will begin to participate in your life. When that happens, supernatural events are going to start happening. It is impossible for them not to. It is impossible for inactivity when God starts to engage you because He is a supernatural being, and that is normal for Him. Things will start happening for you because He is moving into your life and taking over. God is going to do it right for you because He has written certain things about you.

God has certain things written about you that must come to pass, but you have to cooperate with Him. You can cooperate by believing and receiving. You do not doubt or fear; you simply trust God and allow perfect love to drive out fear. Allow the Holy Spirit to reveal love and full acceptance to you because of the blood. Accept that you are fearfully and wonderfully made and that God has a book written about you in Heaven that must come to pass. Angels are ready and on standby to implement God's perfect will into your life.

Before He ever created you to be, He knew you. That is the Jesus I met. That is the Jesus who wrote a book about you, and that is the Jesus I trust. Do not judge God by what you are going through. Judge God by what is written. Seeing that *it's all rigged in your favor* is going to set you free! There is a process of elimination happening in your life, and that elimination is that anything that is not of God is leaving your life. God has brought down the Sword of the Spirit in your life, and He is separating and discerning between what is of you and what is of Him. He is showing it to you right now, and the Spirit of God is convicting you. He is showing you those things that are from Heaven and those that are of the earth, and you are in the process of separating.

When this started happening to me, I started to have angelic visitations. I started having angels come to me. I began having Jesus come to me. I started to be led by the Spirit of God in a greater manner because I let the Lord start to put the Sword in my life and say, "Here is the way you should walk and where you should go. It will help if you let go of this. You need to leave this, and you need to take this on." The Lord began to dictate as I gave Him my heart and allowed the Lord to occupy me. I began to see the manifestation of the supernatural in my life, and I know that is what you want.

YOU HAVE VALUE

Your value down here on earth is determined in Heaven and not determined on the earth. Regardless of how much you work or accomplish on this earth, the value that you have is determined in Heaven. It is based on what God has already determined about you. He invested in you before you were even born. Jesus was the Lamb that was slain before the foundation of the world, according to Revelation 13:8. You were already redeemed in God's mind and heart. He planned for Jesus to come back knowing that you were going to fall and knowing that when you were born you were going to be born into sin. In His love and mercy, He created a way out through Jesus Christ. God has foreknowledge, but He does not make you choose Him. He still lets you do your own thing.

God has all these beautiful things written about you. You still have time to change your direction. If you feel as though you are not as committed as you should be, then you need to have the revelation that *it's all rigged in your favor* and that God has already written out good plans with a good end. He has a purpose for you that is beyond your comprehension. If you can accept this, then you can get rid of rebellion right now, which will allow you to stop resisting God and remove your doubt. Fear, doubt, and unbelief will go, and the Spirit of God can take you into the next stage quickly if you want it. You have to release yourself into your future right now; you must see that you can change things so that you do not have to come up short at the end. The reason that I have written this book is to prevent people from coming up short in their life and not accomplishing the things that they were supposed to. I am breaking the power of the devil over people by doing this. I have been writing and teaching courses to show people that God has already predetermined what He wants to do for people. God still allows people to come up with their own decisions. If I can inform people of the right understanding so that they can make a good decision, then I can assist in the acceleration process and help people to make the right decisions about God.

CLEAR UP MISCONCEPTIONS

God is not doing all these evil things to you. I saw in Heaven that God had nothing to do with the evil. I saw that the devil had been disobedient, had fallen, and took humankind with him. He is the one that is misrepresenting God. The devil hates God and the devil hates you, and he is going to misrepresent God to you. He is going to make God look bad. He is going to make it look like God did things to you, but you know that God had nothing to do with it. God is falsely accused of being a murderer and a liar. God does not lie, and He does not murder. Satan is a murderer, and he is a liar, and he will misrepresent God to people. Clear this up now and get rid of the doubt and the fear by allowing yourself to yield to the truth—the truth that God already wrote a good story about you, and He wants to implement that right now through the angels, the Holy Spirit, and through the revelation of the Word of God. All of these things working together will cause you to triumph in this life. Do not wait until you absolutely need help from God. Get into a relationship with Him now and have intimacy with Him. Do not resist intimacy but accept the Spirit of God, receive the Word of God, and allow the angels to work because the angels are standing by right now to implement your books. They have been permitted to make sure that you are on the same page as God is on today's calendar date.

Your angels have read your book all the way until the end...they just need your cooperation.

You will finish your life in an effective manner when you accept the angelic assistance that has been assigned to you. God's Word concerning you is written in your book in Heaven. Because God, your heavenly Father, loves you and not only has He written about you but He also wants to implement those plans into your life. He does this by bringing your book into manifestation in this physical realm. The psalmist said, *"You saw who you created me to be before I became me! Before I'd ever seen the light of day, the number of days you planned for me were already recorded in your book"* (Ps. 139:16 TPT). As a believer grasps these wonderful truths, you will walk in the fear of the Lord and find favor with God. The prophet Malachi wrote this:

> *Then those who feared the Lord spoke to one another, and the Lord listened and heard them; so a book of remembrance was written before Him for those who fear the Lord and who meditate on His name. "They shall be Mine," says the Lord of hosts, "on the day that I make them My jewels. And I will spare them as a man spares his own son who serves him." Then you shall again discern between the righteous and the wicked* (Malachi 3:16-18).

As you can see, there was a remnant that feared the Lord. The Lord was listening to what they said and had a book written concerning those who practiced the fear of the Lord and meditated on Him. The Lord considers us to be His through ownership. He has plans for us to be put on display as His own private stock. I have seen this truth in the heavenly realms with Jesus. He loves us and will surely keep us by His mighty angels. Jesus said, *"Be careful that you not corrupt one of these little ones. For I can assure you that in heaven each of their angelic guardians have instant access to my heavenly Father"* (Matt. 18:10 TPT).

Please allow the angels to work according to what was written about you before you were born. The angels have much to do with your destiny in this life. Be sure to build your faith up and see your heavenly book fulfilled. In these last days, there will be many supernatural events as God the Father begins to answer the cries of His people through angelic intervention. The angels can see by what is written that *it's all rigged in your favor!*

I remember seeing in Jesus's eyes the love He has for people. He really knows that people don't have to fail. There are so many good things that He has in store for you. Meditate on Him and fear Him; He will come through for you.

Whatever it is that God has planned for you, He wants you to be on the same page with Him. The angels have already been briefed about what should be happening in your life, and they are waiting for you to cooperate. Do that by believing and cultivating your heart with faith and by sowing the Word in your heart. This will cause faith to come up and out of your spirit so you can then speak out your destiny. Know that what you believe and what you say are coming from your heart, and when you say it you know that what you say is going to come to pass and that you shall have it. Then, after speaking in faith and believing, put your feet into action and walk it out; do those things that have been stirred by your faith.

The Lord is with you. He wants you to walk with Him, but He will not make you do it. God has plans that are written, and you are supposed to be walking in those plans because you need to help other people to walk in their plans. The delay is causing other people to not walk in this. If I had not come back, I would not be teaching like this, because prior to meeting Jesus I was not engaging God on that level. Now that I have, I am teaching others to engage in it. My whole goal is not just to help you but to help this entire generation of people.

You are going to be affected by the Word and, in turn, you will go and help other people and change lives everywhere. Those people will then spread it to others until the whole generation is reached. This is how big God's plan is! Listening to God is more important than you think. If you fulfill what has been written in your book and fulfill what God has for you, then those around you will be influenced to fulfill their books.

God made you intricately, and He knew you before you were even in existence. His intention for you is attached to other people. His intention for your life is going to affect a whole generation, and future generations, because of your obedience.

Chapter 10

THE LORD THINKS ABOUT YOU

Every single moment you are thinking of me!
How precious and wonderful to consider that you
cherish me constantly in your every thought!

—Psalm 139:17 TPT

SOMETIMES IT IS HARD TO UNDERSTAND HOW GOD could think about you personally when there are so many people on the earth at one time. However, I have found that He can do that with ease. I remember when I had a deadline with my bank. There was an agreement to transfer money to another account by a certain date so that I would not be penalized interest for the past year. If I did not transfer it by a certain date, I would be penalized five hundred dollars. I was out flying for the airline that I worked for and forgot to transfer the money. In fact, I did not remember it for another two weeks. When I realized my oversight, I prayed and asked the Lord for mercy. Then, I called the bank to ask for mercy as well. I wanted to get them to reverse the $500 penalty against my account. When I got a hold of the lady at the bank, she looked up my records and told me that everything was fine. I asked her what she meant by that. She said, "Well Mr. Zadai, our records show that you did call on the date, and we switched it for you, so everything is fine."

I was so surprised at what the Lord had done, and so I thanked her and hung up very quickly. I then went to prayer and asked the Lord what had just happened. He told me that He had answered my prayer in advance, two weeks ago, because He knew that I would pray. The Lord was thinking about me and answered a prayer that I had not prayed yet!

There is revelation that I received during my visitation with Jesus in 1992 that I am just now being released to share. In this chapter, I am excited to share a few of the secrets and in-depth revelations that I have never shared. In this chapter, I am going to be sharing that the Lord thinks about you. When I was with Jesus, He allowed me at times to hear His thoughts. Other times He would hear my thoughts and answer me without speaking. I was able to look in His eyes and communicate with Him.

Your Choking Point

Psalm 139:17-18 says this: "*Every single moment you are thinking of me! How precious and wonderful to consider that you cherish me constantly in your every thought! O God, your desires toward me are more than the grains of sand on every shore! When I awake each morning, you're still with me*" (TPT). When you get into Psalm 139, it does not take long before you reach your choking point. People do not know that they have a choking point, but they receive so much information and revelation that there is a point when it becomes too difficult to handle. Your mind gets involved, and then you choke on it. In other words, people have a hard time believing certain things that the Bible says.

There comes a point when you must decide as a Christian whether you are going to believe the Bible or not. Some of what the Word says is so exceedingly above and beyond what we can ask or think that it is hard for us to even imagine that these things are true. As a Christian, you must continually make decisions when you read, study, and meditate on the Word.

> *"For My thoughts are not your thoughts, nor are your ways My ways," says the Lord. "For as the heavens are higher than the earth, so are My ways higher than your ways, and My thoughts than your thoughts"* (Isaiah 55:8-9).

When the Lord speaks to you, and when you have encounters with Him, some things are going to make your mind want to click off because the mind cannot comprehend the things of God. There is a point in people's thinking where this usually happens. This verse in Psalm 139 says, *"Every single moment you are thinking of me!"* If you are a Christian, you have to believe the Bible because the Bible is our authority; it is the foundation of what we believe. When people ask you what religion you are, you say, "I am a Christian." Well, a Christian is a Christian because they believe in Jesus Christ, but they also believe in the Word of God as being the foundation. It is the truth from Heaven that was given to us through men and women as the Holy Spirit moved on them and they wrote.

What we have in the Bible is our foundation. If you are a Christian, you are also a believer and student of the Word of God, because that is your basis for what you believe; the doctrine of the Bible is your statement of faith. Here in Psalms, it is saying that every single moment God is thinking of you. Your mind is likely trying to fathom how that is even possible when there are so many people in the world. How can God know everyone's thoughts, keep track of them, and then think of them constantly? The psalmist here is saying that it is so. You have a choice to make. Is the Bible true or not? As a Christian, you have to say yes, and you have to believe it, but this is where the choking point is for most people. They have to accept this, but it is too big to fathom; they cannot comprehend it. In order to receive and accept it, you must adjust your heart to determine that this is true even if you do not see the result of it in your own life. You have to tell your mind that what the Bible says is true and your experience is wrong.

If God is not doing something that He said He would, it is not God's fault; it has to be something else. It may be you. The first thing I do is look at myself to assume the blame. I do not blame God for anything that happens. It is never God's fault. I met Jesus, and He is not capable of failing. The angels that have been assigned to me are not capable of failing. Bad things have happened, and afterward, I have discovered that it was because of me, not God. You must accept when the blame is yours. This is the choking point for most people. They do not want to be accountable for their life decisions. People do not want to commit to anything because they do not want to be responsible. They say that they are a Christian. On paper, they agree to everything, but in reality they do not believe everything in the Bible. Choose to believe and agree that according to the Word God is thinking of you every moment, and He is concerned about you.

If things are not happening correctly in your life, it is because you need to adjust yourself. You must move toward God instead of expecting Him to move toward you. He has done everything He is going to do. When the Father sent Jesus, He completed His end of the deal. Jesus came, repurchased you, sealed it up, and then went back to the Father. Now, God is waiting for His enemies to become His footstool and Jesus is waiting for the church to rise and fulfill her destiny by becoming unified and built up. There is a unity of the faith until we come into maturity, then the Body of Christ will be a witness on the earth. The end will come when the harvest comes. The five-fold ministries and the gifts of the Spirit are given to build up the body.

> *For the equipping of the saints for the work of ministry, for the edifying of the body of Christ, till we all come to the unity of the faith and of the knowledge of the Son of God, to a perfect man, to the measure of the stature of the fullness of Christ* (Ephesians 4:12-13).

GOD'S DESIRES FOR YOU

The psalmist is saying how precious and wonderful to consider this idea that every moment God is thinking of me. God is thinking of you right now. He cherishes you constantly. The psalmist says, "*O God, your desires toward me are more than the grains of sand on every shore! When I awake each morning, you're still with me.*" If you look at how much sand is on just one small portion of the beach and you think that God's desires toward you are as many as the grains of sand on all those shores, your mind is going to go tilt.

Being a Christian is not always easy. You have to understand spiritual truths and take them down in your heart. Spiritual truths cannot be understood in your mind. Your brain may disqualify you from understanding, but your heart will qualify you, and you will respond in faith. Faith is of the heart, not of the head.

When the psalmist awoke every morning, he said that the Lord was still with him no matter what. Think about Adam and Eve and how they sinned by eating of the tree. After that, God came down and wanted to walk with them, and He was looking for them. They were hiding, but God was not hiding. God came down and treated them just the way He had before. What changed? They changed. They changed their position. You have to understand that God wants fellowship. God wants to communicate with His creation. However, when people move away from God, then they suffer in their relationship with Him. God wanted to know where Adam was, and then He asked why he was hiding. God wanted to have Adam explain what happened because He cared about Adam.

The psalmist says that even when he awakes in the morning, God is right there waiting for him. His desires for him are more than the sands that are on the shores of the land. Think about how you feel about yourself. Why do you feel that way you do about yourself? It is because people treated you a certain way. However, the way people treated you was not because they knew you; it was based on what they felt about themselves. How they feel about themselves is how they treat people. They are going to mistreat you because they are wrong, and so they mistreat you wrongly. If you listen to them and take what they say seriously, then you will start to feel bad about yourself and, in turn, treat others wrong if you allow it to transfer. This is a curse and it is something that is transferred down from generation to generation. The only way that you can correct this is to know the thoughts of God toward you and to know that you must be close to Him.

Most people I know do not have the close relationship that they desire with the Lord and do not seem to understand why. It is because they have been mistreated, and they think that God feels the same way about them. It is simply not true. I found this out when I was with Jesus. I have spent much time with Him on several occasions. He never mistreated me in any way. Jesus has brought discipline at times and has been upset with me, but He has never mistreated me. He just wanted the correction to come because He loves me (see Heb. 12:6). Jesus told me things that I did not want to hear but that I needed to hear. There were times when He complimented me, and if I were to share some of the things that Jesus has told me personally many would be jealous and ask why I am special. The truth is that I had counted the cost and because of the right decisions that I made. And this was not based on being recognized by anybody, but what was done in secret. I was commended, and God gave me favor and complimented me, and I have a deeper relationship.

I see that everyone can have that, but not everyone wants to pay the price for it. When the Lord is thinking about you, it will shift you over into this place where you feel accepted, and when you are accepted then you are not rejected. As a result, you do not act out of rejection anymore; you act out of acceptance. The Spirit of God is given as a spirit of adoption (see Rom. 8:15). This verse can be translated as the "Spirit of acceptance." You are accepted because of the blood. Just like adoption, you have been chosen and adopted in and you are treated as though you are lineage, just as a child who is genetically related.

INSIDE THE EYES OF JESUS

The Holy Spirit within you is continually calling out to your Father, and you are accepted. You are not rejected, even though you feel rejected. When I was in Heaven, I realized that in this world there were certain things that I felt that had not been coming from God at all. They were coming from satan, and I did want to come back to this realm because I saw that this verse in Psalms is true. Jesus had thought of me, planned to do these things for me, and then He breathed me into my mother's womb. After He initiated the process, I came out exactly how He thought of me. While I stood with Jesus, He allowed me to walk into His eyes. I went into His eyes, and I watched everything that happened before I was even born. God had ordained for me to be who I am and to do the things that I am doing now. He had ordained it, but up until that point I had not done everything that He desired for me to do. Yet I was going to Heaven, and I was going to be rewarded.

When He sent me back from the dead, I had an opportunity to redo things. In other words, I could do more now. This is why I am producing books, videos, online courses, and preaching all over the world. It is because I have been given another chance to do it right, and I should have discerned this all by the Word of God, but I did not. Now I want to help you.

When I walked into Jesus' eyes, I saw the process in which He thinks of you. He names you, begins forming your body in your mother's womb, and then He breathes your spirit into you, and you become a living person. God wanted you to be born, and He purposed in His heart to create you. He writes in a book all the good things that He plans for you to do.

Whether or not you fulfill the good works that are written in your book has to do with your understanding, your knowledge, and your faith. As you understand things, you begin to do those things that are written in your book. Faith without works is dead—or, faith without action is dead. The action of your faith will allow God's plans to manifest in your life.

It is the same thing with what I saw in Jesus' eyes. I saw that there had to be the manifestation in my life and not just the belief, and when I started to realize that then I understood that He was continually thinking good thoughts of me. He has never doubted me or spoken a bad word about me. He has not put any limitations on me at all. All the limitations that were placed on me were placed on me down here in this earthly realm.

God Himself has never limited me, nor has anybody in Heaven limited me. Jesus told me that there is no one in Heaven limiting you; they all believe in you. The angels that are assigned to you all believe in you and talk about you. The Lord told me that Heaven knows who I am and that I am being talked about. I thought, "You've got to be kidding me." I did not think I was that important, but Jesus said that because of my faith and my character I am integral. He told me that these qualities are rare on the earth, and that if I were to talk to people in Heaven they would know who I was.

It just touched me that the sacrifices that I had made to walk the narrow way also meant that people around the world would know and receive from the ministry that God has called me to. The "narrow way" meant that I was to do things humbly and in secret instead of outwardly. In doing this, there is a risk of never being noticed or promoted, which is what the world teaches us to value. In Matthew 6:4, Jesus said, "*So that your deeds of charity may be in secret; and your Father Who sees in secret will reward you openly*" (AMPC). That takes faith. There are a lot of things that I had done in secret and things that I have done that cost me more because I did it right instead of by manipulating. The Lord had written that down, and He was making it up to me.

SEARCHING THE DEEP THINGS OF GOD

I encourage you that no matter what the world says about your relationship with God, you need to judge it by the fact that God is thinking about you and that He has never doubted you. He is not in any way thinking that you are going to fail. He looks right at you, and He wants to strengthen you and empower you to do His will. He also wants to send angels to help you. So every thought is precious. Everything that He thinks about you is unimaginable, which means that even your mind cannot comprehend it. Now, this gets into what Paul saw when he was caught up in the heavenlies, which he wrote to the Corinthians:

> *"Eye has not seen, nor ear heard, nor have entered into the heart of man the things which God has prepared for those who love Him." But God has revealed them to us through His Spirit. For the Spirit searches all things, yes, the deep things of God* (1 Corinthians 2:9-10).

In this Scripture, Paul was saying that God has done so many good things that it is beyond what we can even comprehend or are ever going to know. However, there is a way to know, and Paul says that it is by the Spirit. The Spirit searches the deep things of God. In the early part of chapter 2, Paul tells the Corinthians that he did not come with the enticing words of man's wisdom, but in power and demonstration of the Holy Spirit (see 1 Cor. 2:1-5). Paul was revealing the fact that even though he was an educated man—"a Pharisee of Pharisees"—having studied under the head Pharisee, that he did not come bearing any of that kind of knowledge and wisdom. Instead, he came in power and demonstration of the Holy Spirit.

I am believing that you will come to understand that you are nothing without the Holy Spirit. The Holy Spirit wants to open the door to the supernatural to you. However, you cannot enter into spiritual things in your physical body or mind; spiritual things must be spiritually discerned. Do not miss this. Do not wait until you are in Heaven to learn how important the Holy Spirit is in your life.

The Holy Spirit has to usher you into your destiny. So, what you are going to find out is that without Him, you can do nothing. You have to have the Holy Spirit to get you in. He will take you through the door. When you go through that door, you are not going to get credit for it. Are you willing to not take credit? The good things that you do will be because the Holy Spirit told you to do them, and not because you had a better way or that you wanted to do it your way.

You cannot be a Spirit-led Christian, walking in the Spirit, and at the same time do your own thing. You cannot even interject your thoughts into it because your thoughts are far from God's thoughts. God's will for your life is spiritual. The book that was written about you before you were born is a spiritually discerned book. You cannot add to the book if you were not even in the meeting when they wrote the book about you! God did not ask for your opinion or your input when they wrote your book. It was based on what God's wisdom said, what He desired for you, and for the generation that you live in. You are going to influence a whole generation even though you think you are so insignificant. God does not think that way. He sees everything written in your book as being part of a whole plan that is affecting an entire generation and even future generations. You are an answer to the previous generation's prayers. Every day there are opportunities to be answering prayers that were prayed previously from Christians who interceded for this generation.

DEMONSTRATION OF GOD'S POWER

God's power is made manifest as wisdom from Heaven. It is a demonstration of the power of God, not of man's wisdom. You must have a connection with the other realm. You can do this by going past your own understanding. You have to go to a place where the Spirit reveals things to you, and then you walk in that revelation.

For instance, it is impossible for a Christian not to give because God gave His only Son, and we have redemption and have been forgiven. That is why Jesus said that because you have been forgiven, you must also forgive. You are asked to forgive no matter what the circumstance because you have been given forgiveness first. It is the same way with everything else in your life. You have certain traits as a Christian that you have to display because God displayed them on your behalf already. You must give, forgive, and love. You have to walk in the Spirit and not in the flesh because Jesus walked in the Spirit and not in the flesh. Jesus drove out devils, and so you have to drive out devils. Jesus laid hands on the sick, and they recovered; you will lay hands on the sick, and they will recover. He said that believers would operate in "the greater works." Not only will we continue the same works as Jesus, but we are also going to do greater works than He did. Jesus raised people from the dead, so you are going to raise the dead. And there will be even greater manifestations of God's power.

There must be a transference of the Spirit for you to go past the threshold of your limitations. The limitations that you are encountering were not put there by God. They were put there by the fall, and they were put there by people who taught you the wrong things. You have to spiritually discern that some of the things you believe are not correct. God is cherishing you, and His thoughts toward you are wonderful and kind, and He is planning good things for you, so you must accept that. His desires toward you are so many and so great that it would overwhelm you. You may say, "I don't feel like that," and that is because you are connected to this earthly realm through the body and the mind and you focus on what you think and feel. All the informational input that is coming to you is coming from your body. It comes from what you can see and hear physically, and what you can think and feel with your mind. Additionally, your emotions and your will are involved.

You are taking everything in, and you are making decisions about yourself based on what data has come in to you. If people mistreat you, then you immediately think that there is something wrong with you, but what if there is actually something wrong with them? Most often, this is the case. People are only going to treat you how they have been treated. Anyone who has the revelation that I have been talking about will not mistreat people at all. They will love people because they've been loved. They have been given patience and forgiveness, and so they are going to give those things back out to others. These people are reminded that they too need help sometimes; that they also need forgiveness and patience. You will notice that this transaction will cause people to go further than they would normally go on their own.

Keep reminding yourself that God is always thinking good thoughts toward you. If you in any way feel that God does not love you or that He is mad at you or has terrible thoughts for you, recognize that the devil is trying to sever your relationship with God. The enemy is trying to get in there and deceive you as a way of separating you from God. That is what he did to Adam and Eve. He made Eve feel as though God was leaving her out of some things, but in truth God was not leaving her out of anything. Eve had everything. She and Adam had God come down and talk to them every day face to face. What was she doing even discussing their relationship with a serpent? There was no need for that. What she should have done was walk away. But she started to talk to him, and when she did, satan was able to manipulate her mind out of what she was told and twist it into something else. And so Eve sinned; she fell. That is what satan is trying to do to you. To make you feel like you are missing out and that God is holding things back from you, and to make you feel that God is mad at you. These are things that satan does in this physical realm and mental realm to try to separate you from God. You must put a stop to that! God loves you. Remember, when you look into the eyes of Jesus, you are only going to see love. You are going to see compassion. You are going to see a God who believes in you!

Chapter 11

THE LORD PROTECTS YOU AS A MIGHTY WARRIOR

*Lord, can't you see how I despise those
who despise you? For I grieve when
I see them rise up against you.*

—PSALM 139:21 TPT

THERE WAS A PARTICULAR SITUATION ONE TIME WHEN the Lord asked me to talk to someone about a difficult subject that required me to bring correction to certain person. I obeyed the Lord but lost that person as a friend because of it. They ended up slandering me to others because they were upset with me. I stayed up all night praying for that person anyway. The next day, I went for a run through a park near my house. All of a sudden, as I was running at a quick pace the Lord Jesus appeared to me as a warrior with a drawn sword. He was dressed in golden armor with red and blue garments underneath. It was an open vision, and I did not even realize that I kept running as I walked up to Him in the vision. He began to speak to me and encourage me, thanking me for my love and obedience toward Him. Jesus told me that because I had taken a stand for Him, He was taking a stand for me as well. At this point, He drew a very large, beautiful sword with gemstones on the handle. He said, "I am going to fight against your enemies because you are standing up for Me." At this point, Jesus turned around and walked off, and I continued my run without missing a step. The Lord wants to fight our battles. Be encouraged that He is with you as a *Mighty Warrior!*

The Lord is going to reveal Himself to you in many ways. I have seen the Lord many times, and in this instance He was dressed differently. I see something different about Him every time. The Lord is going to reveal Himself to you, and there will always be more and new characteristics that He will show you about Himself. He is multifaceted, and there is no way that we will be able to know Him completely. I want to encourage you that as you read this book, God is going to unfold and reveal Himself to you in a new and different way.

> *O God, come and slay these bloodthirsty, murderous men! For I cry out, "Depart from me, you wicked ones!" See how they blaspheme your sacred name and lift up themselves against you, but all in vain! Lord, can't you see how I despise those who despise you? For I grieve when I see them rise up against you. I have nothing but complete hatred and disgust for them. Your enemies shall be my enemies!* (Psalm 139:19-22 TPT)

Part of it being *rigged in your favor* includes the benefits of being a child of God. You inherit whatever your parents have. Whatever they have, you can receive the benefits. When you are growing up, you are under someone's care. When you become a child of God, you have come under the authority of God Almighty, and the Father has done this for us through Jesus Christ. Jesus met all the demands that were required to get us back into fellowship with God.

We are in fellowship with God through the Spirit of God and the blood of Jesus. In your walk with God, you have to get to the place where you begin to realize this and implement it. I want to encourage you that your enemies have now become God's enemies because they have come against you. And the ownership part of this covenant means that that you share in the benefits of God Almighty. If enemies are coming against you, then they are coming against Him also. When Paul got knocked off his horse on the road to Damascus, Jesus said, "Why are you persecuting Me?" Paul's response was, "When did I persecute You, Lord?" Jesus explained that when Paul persecuted the Lord's children, he was also persecuting Jesus.

FREEDOM FROM CURSES

We are now encountering the Father side of God that is in the covenant. He is saying to our enemies, "Listen, if you are picking on them, you are picking on Me, and I am going to protect them." Every day, in your prayers and your confession, you have to acknowledge the fact that God Himself is going to take care of you. If you have anyone coming against you, the Lord is going to go and take care of that.

I saw this happen not that long ago after I realized that I had grown up with a victim mentality. I realized that if I did not start to change and shift with what God had done for me through the covenant, I was going to continue to be a victim. Certain things would happen to me, and it was like a curse. I would attract the curse and attract bad things to happen to me all the time. One day, the Holy Spirit just said, "You need to flip this on the enemy." The Lord showed me that growing up I was picked on. I was left out of things and rejected at certain times. This is common, but the Lord showed me that it can become chronic to the point where there are demonic spirits that are enforcing that curse. If you are having that happen in your life, then I want to talk about that now.

There are demon spirits that are assigned to you even if you do not believe it. You may say, "God is protecting me because I am a Christian." If this were the case, then why would Paul have even talked about warfare, weapons, and the armor that you will need? There is a war, and we show up enforcing what God has given us. We use the weapons that we have been given to put an end to the demonic spirits' ability to impose a curse.

Angels come and they enforce a blessing. If you are following the Lord and have chosen to walk with Him in the power of the Spirit and in the fear of the Lord, then God is going to send angels to you that are going to enforce a blessing. Alternately, there are demon spirits assigned to try to get you off course. They are trying to stop you and stop God from moving in your life. Sometimes you are going to have attacks, but you have to know and understand that this is normal for a Christian to encounter, especially if you are doing anything for God.

I don't often share in-depth about this topic because it is so controversial, but there are strategic attacks planned against you. Attacks that are designed to knock you out of what God has called you to do. Satan has a right to try to test you and try to opt you out by getting you to choose not to serve God. He has the legal right to test your borders and present you with temptations. We know that this is true because we see it every day. Evil spirits will test your borders, trying to find out where your weaknesses are. Paul warned that satan is like a lion that goes around seeking whom he may devour (see 1 Pet. 5:8).

We need to strengthen ourselves. What I found out was that evil spirits will opt out of a fight if they feel that you are too strong for them. You must choose not to be a victim and not expect bad things to happen to you. If something does happen, then right away you must go after those evil spirits and start to address them and drive them out. You call them on their ploys and let them know that you know their strategies against you. You call them on those things and let them know that their battle strategies and ploys are done; they are null and void. When you do this, the evil spirits will leave and find someone weaker. They will see you as not being worth the hassle. Stand your ground in the Lord.

> *Therefore take up the whole armor of God, that you may*
> *be able to withstand in the evil day, and having done all,*
> *to stand* (Ephesians 6:13).

The devil will look you in the eye, and if you have no fear, knowing that you have been called of God and that your Father is protecting you in Heaven, then he will back off because he knows that he cannot have you.

Everyone must go through this. You must face the giant that is confronting you. Stand there and look him right in the eye without any fear and say, "Satan, I have had it with you. I reject everything that you are sending my way, and I drive you out, bind you up, and cast you out!" When you do this and continually reinforce it every day, you will begin to see things turn to the point where there is no curse and you are not a victim anymore. The ultimate destination is to one day arrive at the realization that satan is the victim. Believers need to victimize him continually. Start to enforce this in your life, and you will cease to be a victim. I remember the day that I woke up and I was no longer a victim. When you realize this, he begins to back off and leave you alone.

Do not back down or try to hide. People may feel that they do not want to cause trouble or rile the devil. They believe that he will leave them alone if they leave him alone. This is not so. He will not leave you alone just because you leave him alone. The demons have no way of ever being redeemed or getting back with God because they are lost. You are in the family of God and they are out. Because of that, they cannot win. At times, the demonic activity will appear to be ridiculous in their approach to you because they cannot win. They are going to lose big time, but they are going to go out swinging. You also must come out swinging. You have to wake up every morning and beat the devil over the head with a spiritual two-by-four. You have to go after him.

If you are not seeing things happen, you are being stolen from.

One of the many insights that I gained through revelation of the Spirit of God was the fact that if there was no manifestation after you prayed, you were being stolen from by the enemy. The Lord hears you when you pray, and He begins to answer you from the heavenly realms. Angels are sent and fight against evil forces to get to you. It is very important that you grasp this concept so that you will not give up and be stolen from as angels will break through on your behalf.

I also saw very clearly that things were being held back because the enemy knew that they were God's expression of His love for us. The devil desires to hinder that expression when God sends it to His children. The Lord is always wanting to express His love by revealing Himself and providing as a good Father would. Satan desires to slander God by holding back the provision and the expression of love in the physical realm so that God will be misrepresented and misunderstood.

It is not enough to have your enemy exposed and found out. You must require him to pay you back. According to Proverbs 6:31, *"But if he's caught, he still has to pay back what he stole sevenfold; his punishment and fine will cost him greatly"* (TPT). So do not be discouraged if you encounter warfare concerning your answers. The enemy is trying to steal your joy. Do not allow him to do it. Continue to reinforce what you know to be true because God has not failed you. He is working right now to bring it to pass. Just call the enemy out on his stealing from you and let him know that he must either cease his maneuvers against you or pay the penalty sevenfold.

Jesus showed me in the heavenly visitation in 1992 that we should never give up praying and should diligently reinforce through prayer the revealed will of God given to us by the Word of God and by the Spirit of God. Jesus taught me that we should pray in the Spirit continually, no matter how we feel, because God is working. He is going to come through for you if you do not give up in fervent prayer. So, remember this: it is very important that you do not give up no matter what warfare you encounter because it is already rigged in your favor.

Jesus showed me shockwaves coming from my spirit-being when I prayed, showing that my prayers were effective and that they were going forth and accomplishing the intent of God's heart and my heart. The Spirit of God will confirm God's Word in your life by signs and wonders following you. Just watch and see what He does for you!

Every morning, wake up and hit the devil in the head with a two-by-four just because you can.

In general, there seems to be a fervency in prayer missing in the Body of Christ these days. In times past we find that people knew how to pray with a fervency that the apostle James talked about, *"Confess and acknowledge how you have offended one another and then pray for one another to be instantly healed, for tremendous power is released through the passionate, heartfelt prayer of a godly believer!"* (James 5:16 TPT).

Jesus has taught me to pray from the very depths of my spirit where the Holy Spirit dwells. There is a place where you can yield so that the Holy Spirit has free course to use your mouth to flow out of you like rivers of living water, prophesying into your environment and speaking the truth to where it frames your world. From this place, nothing is impossible and everything that you say, which was spoken by the Spirit of God, will come to pass. Again, you need to yield to the Spirit.

Jesus taught me to allow my environment to be conducive for growth. While I live here on the earth, I must learn to shut out the world, with its desires and thoughts, and focus on the desires and thoughts of God and speak them from my mouth with fervency. This fervency is directly connected to the fire of God at the altar in Heaven. It has to do with the authority that comes from the very throne of God, which backs you up as a child of God speaking by the Spirit.

Sometimes you just have to figuratively pick up that two-by-four and start swinging it at the devil. In other words, you must use blunt force against him. Fervency in prayer does this as well. It is like taking a blunt object to the devil. It is time to do a little warfare and swing the Sword of the Spirit and bring down every high thing that exalts itself against the knowledge of God! Here are two aggressive warfare Scriptures that I meditate on often to remind me of how effectively God protects me. Remember, you are a potent ambassador of the Kingdom of God:

> *For though we walk in the flesh, we do not war according to the flesh. For the weapons of our warfare are not carnal but mighty in God for pulling down strongholds, casting down arguments and every high thing that exalts itself against the knowledge of God, bringing every thought into captivity to the obedience of Christ, and being ready to punish all disobedience when your obedience is fulfilled* (2 Corinthians 10:3-6).

> *For we have the living Word of God, which is full of energy, and it pierces more sharply than a two-edged sword. It will even penetrate to the very core of our being where soul and spirit, bone and marrow meet!*

It interprets and reveals the true thoughts and secret motives of our hearts (Hebrews 4:12 TPT).

When you get the revelation that you are an ambassador representing Jesus Christ on this earth, you will start to walk into greater authority. Deliverance will come to many people because you speak from the place of deliverance. Healing will come because you speak from the very place of healing. The truth will be made known as you speak from the truth that the Holy Spirit has already placed within you. It comes out like fire from the altar of God. It comes out with authority that comes from the throne of God. It manifests as though God Himself is speaking it because you are His ambassador and you are speaking God's will that is written in Heaven. That is why you must prophesy from the very place where it was first spoken and thought of—the very throne of God. If God is not speaking, you do not speak. But if He *is* speaking, you must speak or be consumed by the fire that first caused those words to be birthed. Jeremiah the prophet experienced this: *"If I say, I will not make mention of [the Lord] or speak any more in His name, in my mind and heart it is as if there were a burning fire shut up in my bones. And I am weary of enduring and holding it in; I cannot [contain it any longer]"* (Jer. 20:9 AMPC).

He tried to keep quiet and not prophesy, but the fire of God wanted to consume him. So he had to prophesy just like you must prophesy because it's already rigged in your favor.

One of the characteristics of demons that I noticed when I was on the other side with Jesus was that they do not think that they are going to get caught. When they do things, they do not have alternate plans for if they fail. Therefore, it is very important that believers concentrate on their spiritual perception. Your spiritual eyesight and discernment are of the utmost importance, especially in these last days with all the deception that is running through the church and in the world. God has plans that cannot fail and always has a way out of everything for you to succeed, so there is a way to escape even if you cannot see it. When the enemy attempts to seduce or tempt you, God always has a plan and a way out of everything. The devil does not count on you figuring out his "mode of operation."

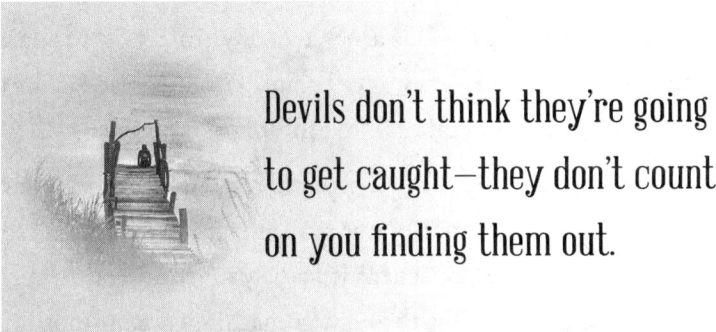

Devils don't think they're going to get caught—they don't count on you finding them out.

The apostle Paul reminded us that the Lord would deliver us from the enemy's trials and temptations in a letter to the Corinthian church. He says:

> *For no temptation (no trial regarded as enticing to sin),*
> *[no matter how it comes or where it leads] has overtaken*
> *you and laid hold on you that is not common to man*
> *[that is, no temptation or trial has come to you that is*
> *beyond human resistance and that is not adjusted and*
> *adapted and belonging to human experience, and such as*
> *man can bear]. But God is faithful [to His Word and to*
> *His compassionate nature], and He [can be trusted] not*
> *to let you be tempted and tried and assayed beyond your*
> *ability and strength of resistance and power to endure,*
> *but with the temptation He will [always] also provide*

the way out (the means of escape to a landing place), that you may be capable and strong and powerful to bear up under it patiently (1 Corinthians 10:13 AMPC).

VICTORY OVER TEMPTATION

You can see that God already knows everything that is to come your way. The Lord makes your victory a sure thing when you allow the faithfulness of a loving heavenly Father to come in like a Mighty Warrior into your life and make a way of escape. Here are some things to consider when the enemy comes in to tempt and test you:

First, you must establish the fact that there is no temptation or trial that will come to you that is not common to every man. No matter how it comes to you or where it leads you, you need to rest assured that you are not going through something uncommon or beyond your ability to bear.

Second, you must also establish the fact that God is faithful. God can be trusted to keep you through any trouble or temptation that may come your way.

Last, you must be fully convinced of the Lord's power and ability to deliver you. His power is always available so that you can endure any situation that you face. Almighty God is much stronger than what you are going through, and He will provide for you an escape so that you can withstand under pressure and come out victorious through any trial or temptation.

1. Spiritual Discernment

Discernment: The act of discerning; also, the power or faculty of the mind, by which it distinguishes one thing from another, as truth from falsehood, virtue from vice; acuteness of judgment; power of perceiving differences of things or ideas, and their relations and tendencies (Webster's Dictionary, 1828).

There is a part of man that can see and hear spiritual things. The Bible refers to it as the "spirit of man." There are three parts to man according to First Thessalonians. The apostle Paul said:

> *Now, may the God of peace and harmony set you apart, making you completely holy. And may your entire being—**spirit, soul, and body**—be kept completely flawless in the appearing of our Lord Jesus, the Anointed One* (1 Thessalonians 5:23 TPT).

The apostle Paul explains that a person's spirit can perceive the thoughts of that person. *"After all, who can really see into a person's heart and know his hidden impulses except for that person's spirit? So it is with God. His thoughts and secrets are only fully understood by his Spirit, the Spirit of God"* (1 Cor. 2:11 TPT). The thoughts of man are a part of the soul of man, which is your mind, will, and emotions. The soul does not discern the spirit realm because it is separate from a person's spirit. The soul and the spirit are so intricately tied together that they are very hard to tell apart at times.

We need to allow the Holy Spirit to give us the ability to discern evil spirits and their operations. The Word and Spirit of God will help us mature in this area. The Word of God is a person named Jesus and He has a sharp Sword coming out of His mouth. Revelation 1:16 says, *"In his right hand he held seven stars, and out of his mouth was a sharp, double-edged sword. And his face was shining like the brightness of the blinding sun!"* (TPT).

Spiritual discernment will become sharper as we allow the Word and the Spirit of God to divide between the soul and the eternal spirit, to allow us to see what is of God and what is of the flesh, the soul, and the evil one.

> *For we have the living Word of God, which is full of energy, and it pierces more sharply than a two-edged sword. It will even penetrate to the very core of our being where soul and spirit, bone and marrow meet! It interprets and reveals the true thoughts and secret motives of our hearts* (Hebrews 4:12 TPT).

2. Spiritual Perception

> Perception: (Latin perceptio) The act of perceiving or of receiving impressions by the senses; or that act or process of the mind which makes known an external object. In other words, the notice which the mind takes of external objects (Webster's Dictionary, 1828).

Being able to perceive what is going on around you is vitally important, not only in this physical realm but in the spiritual realm as well. We always need to be situationally aware of our spiritual environment to discern what the enemy is devising against God's people. Remember, the enemy does not anticipate you being able to see him. Let him know that you can see him and that it is time for him to pay for all that he has done against you and God.

As a believer, Jesus Christ has come into your life, so you need to yield to that light, which will cause you to perceive and understand spiritual things in a clear manner. The unredeemed non-Christian and sometimes the carnal Christian (one who is redeemed yet walks not according to the Spirit but according to the flesh) are not walking with God and need spiritual perception. These people have their understanding darkened, and they cannot see or hear what the Spirit of the Lord is saying to them.

*Their moral understanding is darkened and their reasoning is beclouded. [They are] alienated (estranged, self-banished) from the life of God [with no share in it; this is] because of the ignorance (the want of knowledge and **perception**, the willful blindness) that is deep-seated in them, due to their hardness of heart [to the insensitiveness of their moral nature]* (Ephesians 4:18 AMPC).

Because Jesus has opened our spiritual perception by His Spirit in the new birth, we can see and distinguish between spiritual entities, as well as their purpose and mission. God wants you to distinguish between what is of Him and what is of the enemy. You can then expose the devil and his cohorts and drive them out. Let your perception increase as you yield to your Mighty Counselor, the Spirit of God.

3. *Spiritual Understanding*

Understanding: The faculty of the human mind by which it apprehends the real state of things presented to it, or by which it receives or comprehends the ideas which others express and intend to communicate. The understanding is called also the intellectual faculty. It is the faculty by means of which we obtain a great part of our knowledge. See Luke 24:45, Ephesians 1:18.

1. Comprehending; apprehending the ideas or sense of another, or of a writing; learning or being informed.

2. (adjective) Knowing; skillful. He is an understanding man (Webster's Dictionary, 1828).

In my heavenly vision in 1992 (see my book *Heavenly Visitation*), Jesus continually taught me while I was with Him during an operation. He is such a good teacher as He spoke to me with great authority. One of the personality traits I noticed about Him was that He was concerned that I grasped and understood what He was saying and not just listening to it. It was explained to me that it's not enough to just hear the Word of God. Jesus and the Holy Spirit wanted me to understand and grasp the truth concerning the subjects that He discussed with me. I was told that it is not just what you hear but what you walk away with and understand. Then you must implement that truth into your life. This understanding is what counts when you are in an emergency or in a time of need with how you respond. Having spiritual understanding is to know what God's heart is for any situation and implement it without hesitation in your life.

> *This superabundant grace is already powerfully working in us, **releasing within us all forms of wisdom and practical understanding**. And through the revelation of the Anointed One, he unveiled his secret desires to us—the hidden mystery of his long-range plan, which he was delighted to implement from the very beginning of time. And because of God's unfailing purpose, this detailed plan will reign supreme through every period of time until the fulfillment of all the ages finally reaches its climax—when God makes all things new in all of heaven and earth through Jesus Christ* (Ephesians 1:8-10 TPT).

Whatever you are going through presently, the enemy doesn't expect you to see him and expose his evil works against you. Act as if you know he is there and tell him he has been exposed. Evil spirits don't count on you to see them. You will see the armies of evil begin to retreat as you stand your ground. You can do this. It is all rigged in your favor.

KINGDOM DOMINION

I am telling you this because everyone on this earth is either a victim or a ruler. You are either in charge and ruling and reigning, or you are a victim. There is no in-between. When I was in Heaven, I saw that you are either a victim or you are ruling and reigning as a king. Man was made to rule and reign and to take care of God's earth for Him. God was able to give Adam and Eve dominion over the earth, which was dominion over everything. Now, we have dominion in the name of Jesus. We tell the devil what to do, and then angels come and they assist us. They assist us in our ruling and reigning and in walking in the blessing of God. Most Christians are not blessed because they have not taken dominion. Believers have not turned it around on the devil to where they are the victor and not the victim.

Believers reign above evil spirits and they are to call the shots. If you do not call the shots, evil spirits will. Someone needs to be in charge, and I don't think that any Christian should let the enemy be in charge. The time has come for satan and all his demons to find out who the sons and daughters of God are on the earth! They need to start getting a full dose of the glory of God on a son and a daughter. The Lord is going to protect you as a warrior, but He wants you to turn the battle.

You must have revelation and you need to have the Spirit of God come upon you and enlighten you to where you see these things that I am describing. Paul prays the following for the Ephesians:

> *I pray that the Father of glory, the God of our Lord Jesus Christ, would impart to you the riches of the Spirit of wisdom and the Spirit of revelation to know him through your deepening intimacy with him.*

I pray that the light of God will illuminate the eyes of your imagination, flooding you with light, until you experience the full revelation of the hope of his calling—that is, the wealth of God's glorious inheritances that he finds in us, his holy ones!

I pray that you will continually experience the immeasurable greatness of God's power made available to you through faith. Then your lives will be an advertisement of this immense power as it works through you! This is the mighty power that was released when God raised Christ from the dead and exalted him to the place of highest honor and supreme authority in the heavenly realm! And now he is exalted as first above every ruler, authority, government, and realm of power in existence! He is gloriously enthroned over every name that is ever praised, not only in this age, but in the age that is coming!

And he alone is the leader and source of everything needed in the church. God has put everything beneath the authority of Jesus Christ and has given him the highest rank above all others. And now we, his church, are his body on the earth and that which fills him who is being filled by it! (Ephesians 1:17-23 TPT)

There is a spirit of wisdom and revelation coming upon you, and you are going to understand that you are seated with Christ in heavenly places. You will start to understand that the power that raised Jesus from the dead is dwelling in you, and it is quickening you right now. You are going to start to understand these things by the Spirit of wisdom and revelation.

In addition to revelation, you must get to the point where God visits you. It's where you will feel an anointing as He anoints you. You will receive prophetic utterance. The anointing can be felt upon you and you can speak from it, or it could come up from within you and you begin to speak out. There is the Spirit upon, and then there is the Spirit within.

REVELATION, VISITATION, AND HABITATION

You have to go from *revelation* to the *visitation*, and then eventually you will come to a *habitation*, which is the glory of God. The glory of God is so powerful that when you encounter, it your very personality and everything about you starts to adhere to God's character. You begin to speak, and it is as though you can hear Jesus' voice within your voice and demons know that. When you speak, you are not speaking from this physical realm. You are speaking from the other realm, and this is what we should all be doing.

I know that this may be a big step for some people, but you have to understand something. I did not want to come back, but I did. When I was in Heaven, I saw everything the way it should be. Now that I am back, you must understand that I am going to tell you the truth and I am not going to hold back.

I have come back to encourage and minister, as well as to disciple people and bring them into the fullness of the Spirit. I want people to walk in the power of God themselves, and the Lord wanted me to replicate in other people what He gave me so that they can walk in it as well. That is what I am asking for—that you begin to receive the impartation from the Lord. You need to have a revelation of the Spirit that leads to visitation and then to habitation.

The habitation part of it is when the glory of God comes and you speak *from* the glory. When you have a revelation, you have the anointing upon you and within you, and that anointing teaches you to have the Holy Spirit with you. But when you have visitation, it is a deluge of either the rivers of living water coming out of you or the river deluge coming on you. This is what visitation is like and you can walk in it and speak from it.

However, I am telling you that the day is coming very soon when the Lord as a Warrior is going to bring the glory of the Father into the services and into individual lives. When you go to a church service, you should be walking into the glory and not just into a visitation or revelation. We have gone through those stages in some churches, but we are getting into this next phase, which is a big one called "the glory of God." This is a move of the Spirit where Father God comes into the services and shifts things. People will not need hands laid on them. The power of God will orchestrate the whole service in such a way that the glory of God creates seamless transitions and we go from worship to the message and back into worship. We are getting ready for it and it is coming very shortly.

Back to the idea of not being a victim—you are not a victim in the glory. There are no victims in the glory of God. There are only victors, rulers, those who reign, kings and priests and children of God who walk in that reality. That is what you have to look forward to. When the Lord comes in, He protects you as a Mighty Warrior, but He is also going to disciple you. Even when you feel like you are alone and things are going wrong, you stand up and say, "No! I am a child of God, and God is with me, and I am calling the shots here!" Those demon spirits will leave you alone and clear the area out. You must rule and reign with Jesus.

YOU ARE NOT ALONE

This is the time to meditate and understand the Scriptures. Look up all the Scriptures that talk about being "in Him." The apostle Paul tells about a revelation he had when he was caught up into the heavenlies and saw things that will give understanding to what I am talking about. I saw these things in Heaven, so my spirit has already experienced the next life.

Now that I have come back, I am living in these realities even though I am dealing with all the limitations of this realm. Through the years, I had to decide that I am not a victim anymore. And *we* are not going to be victims anymore. *It's all rigged in your favor*; God has set it up so that He shows up as a Warrior who is going to fight your battles. He is going to war with your enemies, and you are going to fight alongside Him and reinforce the victory.

After you receive revelation and the visitation of the Spirit, you enter into habitation. When this happens, you can walk in the glory all the time. You do not let people or circumstances knock you out of it. There is a sweet spot that you have to stay in with the Holy Spirit and listen to what He is saying and doing. You learn how to control your environment and not let people in who are going to knock you out. What this means is that you are supposed to walk in the Spirit and not in the flesh.

Paul said that those who walk in the Spirit are sons of God. He goes on to say that if you walk in the flesh, you cannot please God. If you walk in that carnal nature, you cannot please God because He said that the flesh is an enemy of the Spirit (see Rom. 8:6-14). The real fight is in the flesh. Your spirit is built up because you are born again, and God's Spirit lives within your spirit. However, your flesh and your soul (the mind, will, and emotions), fight against spiritual things because they are unable to participate in them. Those parts of you want attention and you must learn to not give it to them. To do so, you must focus on the things above, where Christ is seated at the right hand of God.

> *If then you were raised with Christ, seek those things which are above, where Christ is, sitting at the right hand of God. Set your mind on things above, not on things on the earth* (Colossians 3:1-2).

Set your sights high in the Lord and see Him up there as a Warrior. He is a Warrior with a sword, and He is fighting your battles for you. He has declared victory in your life. He already wrote books about you in Heaven, setting it up for you to win. *It's all rigged in your favor.* If you are not winning, it is just because you do not understand the battle that you are in down here. Satan is going to appeal to your flesh and your soul. He will get you into your emotions and your reasoning. His tactic is to draw your attention away from spiritual things.

However, your spirit will see spiritual things. Even now, your spirit man inside of you knows and sees things that your physical eyes do not understand, and your physical ears do not hear what your spirit is hearing. If you would start to focus and develop your spirit, then you would see that the Lord has a drawn sword and He is fighting your battles for you. You would see that the angels have been sent for you to win—not to be a victim, but to be a victor. You can see these things in the spirit.

If you were to read your book, you would see all the beautiful things in there, and you would see what is happening in your life. You would see that you are being promoted. You would see that His glory is going to open up for you. You will see that you are receiving breakthrough. Some people go their whole life and do not see these things happen that are written down about them. It is so sad because it is satan who keeps them in a small place. They do not have a revelation or a visitation, and neither do they have a habitation.

That will not be the case with you! The Spirit of God is visiting you even now. I can sense His power, and I am telling you by the Spirit of God that you have nothing to worry about if you will see that God has designed all of this before you were born. It is an intricate chess game where you win. God has reserved those last moves for you. You can defeat satan every time he comes against you. You can do this, and you can live this life successfully. You can walk it out as *you are not alone*—God is with you. There are many who also believe like this—those who have been taught properly who know the will of God and understand what the Bible says.

Meditate on and rehearse what has been said in this chapter. The Lord is a Warrior who protects you, and He sends angels to minister to you. Psalm 91 says that He assigns angels with special orders to protect you and lift you so that you do not even bump your foot on a stone.

> *I say then: Walk in the Spirit, and you shall not fulfill the lust of the flesh* (Galatians 5:16).

God has all these amazing things planned for you. Begin to think about what it is that God has planned for you. Talk to God about His plans. Pray this: *"Lord, I would like to know Your book and what it says about me. I would like to be effective and productive in this life. Can You teach me?"*

The Holy Spirit will start to accommodate that prayer request by answering you. He will begin to open your eyes and you will start having dreams and visions at night. It began happening to me with dreams, and then people during the day would begin confirming what I was seeing in the spirit at night.

Everything that is in this life is for one thing—to know God more. The more that you know Him, the more you want to do for Him because He has a plan for you. It is not about just understanding God; it's about doing the works of the Holy Spirit and allowing Him to work and manifest through you. Paul said:

> *And I, brethren, when I came to you, did not come with excellence of speech or of wisdom declaring to you the testimony of God. For I determined not to know anything among you except Jesus Christ and Him crucified. I was with you in weakness, in fear, and in much trembling. And my speech and my preaching were not with persuasive words of human wisdom, but in demonstration of the Spirit and of power, that your faith should not be in the wisdom of men but in the power of God* (1 Corinthians 2:1-5).

Paul knew that it was not just about wisdom. It was not just about good words and a good talk. It was the power of the Holy Spirit. To get to that place, we have to walk in the Spirit and not fulfill the lusts of the flesh. God is going to be exalted in your life because you turn the tables on the enemy and you become the victor and the ruler of your life. You are to declare, "I rule and reign as a king in this life. Satan, you are a victim because Jesus defeated you. Jesus destroyed you on the cross and made a show of you openly according to Scripture."

You begin to speak like that, and those devils will leave. I felt devils leaving you right when I wrote those words. There are harassing devils buffeting you even now and they have been trying to harass you.

> *In the name of Jesus, I break every power, and I command every evil spirit to let go of you in the name of Jesus. The Lord protect you. He is your warrior, and He is turning you into a warrior. He is changing you from a victim to a victor. He is turning the tables on the enemy.*

The enemy has to flee because you have submitted to God and you resisted the devil. The word *resist* means to push back. So that is what you are doing—you are pushing back against the devil. You are resisting him. The Word says that he will flee from you in terror (see James 4:7). He is afraid of you!

Chapter 12

THE LORD SEARCHES YOUR HEART

God, I invite your searching gaze into my heart.
Examine me through and through; find out
everything that may be hidden within me.

—PSALM 139:23 TPT

BE ENCOURAGED! THE SPIRIT OF THE LORD IS MINIS-
tering to people through this book, and I can feel His power
so strongly. The Lord searches your heart. He knows exactly
what you are going through, and He is going to encourage
you through His Word. The psalmist prays:

> *God, I invite your searching gaze into my*
> *heart. Examine me through and through;*
> *find out everything that may be hidden within*
> *me. Put me to the test and sift through all my*
> *anxious cares. See if there is any path of pain*

193

I'm walking on, and lead me back to your glorious, everlasting ways—the path that brings me back to you (Psalm 139:23-24 TPT).

The concept of it "being rigged" is that God strategically plans our lives ahead of time before we are even born. It is incredible how it is a narrow path, and Jesus said that only a few find the way to life. I know that for a fact, but I have to get it across to people down here. And how I do that is I encourage people to start to think about a God who does not fail, a God who is not bound by the limitations that we know of in this earth realm. He did not fall. Man fell on the earth, but God did not fall. He is just as He was before He created man.

God's Plan for Man

God knew that man was going to fall, and He planned a redemption through Jesus Christ. Jesus agreed to come and purchase mankind back for the Father before They even created man. I know that is hard to wrap your mind around, but I saw in Heaven that They did not create man without a will. Instead, They created a man with a will so that They would be worshiped, adored, and honored by a person who wanted to do so.

Many people do not want to serve God. They have their ideas about God and about how to live their lives. Even Christians have their opinions about what they believe, and they do not stick with the Word of God. These people have their ideas and push them onto others. There are Christians who manipulate. They do not pray and ask God to help them; instead, they get in there and manipulate people and situations. In Heaven, there is nothing like that at all, so I was sent back to teach people to live according to the Word of God. Do not say something that is not in the Word of God.

Something that does not get enough focus is the fact that God knows everything and that He searches our hearts. Instead, people think, "If God wants me to do this, then He will make me do it." Others may say, "This will work out if it is God's will." If that were indeed the case, then we would have never fallen in the Garden of Eden. God would have taken away that choice and our free will, and we would have just served God and been happy. However, we do have a will. Adam and Eve chose to eat the fruit in the Garden. They decided to do that even though God had said not to. He created man to have free will.

We are going to have temptation in this world, and we are going to have things that happen that are not right. You must be discerning. You cannot just say, "Well, God knows everything, so if He wants it, He can do it." God searches our heart, He looks into our heart, and He knows our heart. He completely understands us. Even now, God understands everything about you, everything that you are going through. He is looking directly into your heart right now. God knows the truth about everything. However, He does not do anything about that unless you are willing to yield to Him.

The Holy Spirit is taking you on a journey, causing you to triumph. He is causing you to overcome fear, overcome disease, overcome every type of addiction, and overcome the devil in every way. If you do not yield to this process, it is because of your self-will. You have to yield to the Greater One who is in you. Jesus sent the Spirit of God, and He is inside of you. He is the Greater One.

It is good that the Lord looks into our hearts and understands us. However, you still have to decide to serve and follow Him. Many people say, "I want to hear God's voice." But you have to be honest with yourself—if you did hear God's voice, would you listen to it? He may say something that you do not expect or that you do not want.

What if God does talk to you. Do you want to hear what He has to say?

WILLINGNESS AND OBEDIENCE

There are times when people do not get what they ask for, and they do not follow God or do the right thing. Why is this? It is because they are not willing to genuinely yield.

> *"If you are willing and obedient, you shall eat the good of the land; but if you refuse and rebel, you shall be devoured by the sword"; for the mouth of the Lord has spoken* (Isaiah 1:19-20).

You may tell the Lord that you are obedient, but are you willing? Are you willing and obedient? This verse in Isaiah explains that we have to be coached into doing the right thing because of the force of the will. If not, then you are going to be like the world and say, "Whatever will be, will be," but no Christian should say that. A Christian should know what the Word of God says and then declare it in their lives. You have to enforce it because satan is not just going to sit back.

The Lord is looking into a person's heart, like yours, and He is examining it through and through. He sees everything, but it should not just stop there. Psalm 139 says, "*find out everything that may be hidden within me.*" There are things in your heart that you do not know or understand about yourself. The psalmist goes a step further than most people are comfortable with, and he asks God to show everything and expose even the wrong things.

When we are obedient *and* willing, God can move us forward. In Mark 10:17, the rich young ruler told Jesus that he was good and had followed the Ten Commandments since his youth and questioned what else he was missing. Jesus loved him, and said, *"One thing you lack: Go your way, sell whatever you have and give to the poor, and you will have treasure in heaven; and come, take up the cross, and follow Me"* (Mark 10:21).

Jesus wanted to take his willingness a step further; He was going to graduate him to the next level. The rich man could not do that because he had learned to depend upon his wealth, and it had become his god. Jesus was asking him to give it up and trust Him, but the man could not do it. Instead, he put his trust in his riches. Many of you have to learn how to yield to what God is saying, and you must be willing. Not just obedient, but willing also.

When God speaks, you can immediately be willing and obedient to do it. The Lord searches you, and He shows you what is hidden. The psalmist wanted to go to the next level and he cried out, *"Put me to the test and sift through all my anxious cares. See if there is any path of pain I am walking on"* (Ps. 139:23-24 TPT).

After Jesus' miracle of multiplying the loaves and fish to feed the five thousand, He spoke to His followers and said that they were only following Him because they had been fed and saw the miracles that He had performed. Then He said something profound; He said, from now on, "If you want any part of Me you have to drink My blood and eat My flesh, or you will not be of Me" (see John 6:26,53-57). Nearly every one of His followers left Him that day except for His disciples. When He asked the disciples if they would leave too, Peter replied, "Where would we go? You have the words of eternal life." They were glued to Him even though they did not understand everything, but you see, Jesus was ready to take the people to the next level.

ALLOWING HIM TO SEARCH
YOUR HEART

Many of us are in pain from past trauma. You may not even know it, but part of your personality is in survival mode because of those situations that have happened in the past. You will notice that there are certain instances when you are hesitant, and you do not trust anymore. It is because you have encountered things and people that have taught you that you cannot operate in trust, and there are certain things that you cannot do anymore. These situations or traumatic events have placed limitations on you.

There is fear involved in this. You begin to fight anxiety, and you do not understand yourself. You may think, "Why do I respond this way, and why do I feel rejected?" Because you experienced trauma, your will has been influenced, and you want to stay in a survival mode. However, the Lord comes in and He searches your heart and exposes those areas. Demons can attach themselves to your soul— your mind, will, and emotions that have not been redeemed.

Your soul is not saved but your spirit is saved because that is the spiritual part of you. The Holy Spirit goes into your spirit and makes you brand new.

> *Therefore, if anyone is in Christ, he is a new creation; old things have passed away; behold, all things have become new* (2 Corinthians 5:17).

This verse in Second Corinthians describes the born-again experience, which is a spiritual experience. However, your psychological, soulish part is a separate part of you.

> *And do not be conformed to this world, but be transformed by the renewing of your mind, that you may*

prove what is that good and acceptable and perfect will of God (Romans 12:2).

You need to be transformed. This is done by meditating on the Word of God. The Word is what begins to change your emotions and influence the way that you think. The soul processes events through thoughts and filters. Because of traumas, your soul has created barriers. In this verse that we are looking at in Psalm 139, the Lord is trying to show us here that *it's all rigged in your favor.* Ask the Lord to sift through all your anxious cares to help you to understand why you are anxious and worried and why you feel this way.

I did this and began to process through it. I found out that because of traumatic events in my life, I was reacting like a victim. I was trying to protect myself because it was just inside of my psychological makeup. It was not me but was just a reaction to fear. To participate in a life *rigged in your favor,* you must allow the Lord to come in and shine His spotlight on your heart and start to show you that there are things in there that are not what God has intended for you.

RESTORING YOUR PATH OF PAIN

You have restrictions placed on you because of the way you were brought up. There are even doctrinal issues where we have been taught wrongly. People interpreted the Bible in a certain way, and it was wrong. These doctrinal issues place limitations on you. If you are unable to believe God for certain things, it is a result of your doctrine. You need to find out what God says in His Word and get back to the Bible as the foundation of all truth.

So, when the Lord says "I am your healer," then that is the truth. Jesus went around healing everyone who was oppressed of the devil.

We know, so we do not have to ask if it's God's will to heal us. The Scripture clearly says that Jesus came to heal people. He did not come to make people sick. He never made anyone sick. When Jesus addressed the people, He told them that they were following Him because of the manifestations. They saw, and they were fed. The people were just spectators.

Jesus told them that He was done with spectators. He wanted someone who would participate in the supernatural. I believe that I came back from Heaven to help people learn how to yield to the Spirit to the point where they turn and are no longer merely spectators.

Is there is any path of pain that you are encountering? If you feel pain inside your heart right now it is because someone has hurt you or situations have hurt you. You have been disappointed and discouraged. You have experienced trauma, and it is valid. It may be that satan had someone do something to you. Because of that attack, you go through your days in pain and hurt and wonder why that happened to you.

It was a satanic attack. You were attacked because of your calling and because of what is written in Heaven about you. So, if there is a path of pain, we need do as the psalmist did in our verse and say, *"God, I invite your searching gaze into my heart. Examine me through and through; find out everything that may be hidden within me. See if there is any path of pain I'm walking on, and lead me back to your glorious, everlasting ways—the path that brings me back to you"* (Ps. 139:24 TPT).

Most people are walking in the way of pain, and because of that the Lord needs to take you by the hand and lead you back into the glory, into healing, deliverance, oneness, adoption, and acceptance. You have full acceptance in the blood. You are not rejected, and God certainly has not rejected you. He has given you everything that you need for life and godliness. God has given you precious promises so that, through them, you can be partakers of the divine nature.

> *Grace and peace be multiplied to you in the knowledge of*
> *God and of Jesus our Lord, as His divine power has given*
> *to us all things that pertain to life and godliness, through*
> *the knowledge of Him who called us by glory and virtue,*
> *by which have been given to us exceedingly great and pre-*
> *cious promises, that through these you may be partakers*
> *of the divine nature* (2 Peter 1:2-4).

We are encountering the supernatural when we yield to the truth. We are walking in the divine nature and those precious promises. The divine nature is a supernatural thing. The apostle Paul said, *"'Eye has not seen, nor ear heard, nor have entered into the heart of man the things which God has prepared for those who love Him.' But God has revealed them to us through His Spirit. For the Spirit searches all things, yes, the deep things of God"* (1 Cor. 2:9-10).

The Spirit is ministering to us and telling us what is hidden. When God reveals things, they come out. They are mysteries until they are revealed. By the Spirit, God wants to take your hand and walk you back in. Not on the path of pain, but on the path where there is glory.

God says, "I am going to lead you back into the glorious, ever-lasting ways" (see Ps. 139:24 TPT). That is what you want. You do not have to wait to get to Heaven to live your life in victory. I saw in Heaven that this was all given to me through Jesus Christ. Now, the only person who taught on this more than anyone else besides Jesus (see John 14–17) was Paul. He talked about this in almost every letter that he wrote, and he wrote almost the entire New Testament.

God wants to bring us back into this glory and into the glorious path where there are everlasting ways. Through his letters, Paul has given us enough revelation to be able to walk in this glorious path right now. Jesus, in John 14–17, also taught us how to stay connected in the vine in the Spirit of God.

> *I am the vine, you are the branches. He who abides in Me, and I in him, bears much fruit; for without Me you can do nothing* (John 15:5).

The Lord is saying, "You can do all things with Me, but without Me, you can do nothing." You see, there has to be a mentality where you are yielding to God and you depend upon Him to help you and allow Him to lead you back.

I can sense the power of the resurrection right now. Healing is coming to you. Your loving heavenly Father is showing you that there is a path of hurt that you are on and that you need to come to the pathway of glory and eternity. Right now, you must start walking in victory, healing, and deliverance! You don't have to be addicted to anything anymore. You can break that power in the name of Jesus!

There is a shift that happens in your heart where you become willing. You are not just obedient, but you are willing to walk and yield in all these areas. The Lord searches your heart and is then able to tell you what He found, and then you can deal with it. Do not resist but be accountable. Tell God, "I am ready for You to speak, and I am prepared to handle what You are going to show me even if it is something that needs to be removed from my life. I am willing."

If this will become your heart's prayer, God will start to show you things. You will instantly know that you need to get rid of something or give something up. At the end of Psalm 139:24, the psalmist writes, *"the path that brings me back to you"* (TPT). Many of us have been led astray because of our hurts. You can be healed today of those hurts and get back on track with the Lord to where you trust Him again. When bad things happen, the first thing we think is, "What have I done to deserve this. Why did God let this happen?"

We feel as though we must process what has happened and file it somewhere and have an explanation. It does not always work out that way. Some of the things that have happened to me, I still do not have an answer about. We are in a fallen world, and we have a devil that hates us. There are fallen spirits that are working against God. You inherited God's enemies when you became a child of God.

Evil spirits fight you like they fight God, but they will also run away from you. They run away from you because they are fearful of God, and they know who you are. They also know when you have come into the knowledge of who you are. This book is meant to build you up to the place where you can begin to use your authority and walk in it.

It is not a human authority. You are not trying to "put your foot down" and be authoritative. It happens when you know that you know that you know that you are an adopted child of God and that you have authority. It happens when you mention your Father's name, and mention your brother Jesus' name, and demons have to listen to you. They are afraid of what you can do to them if you know how to do it.

AN IMAGE OF HEAVEN

The path that we are on now is not the path of hurt. You are walking in the glory. Imagine that you could go to your future and encounter what it is going to be like in Heaven. Imagine being at the end. This is where I was. What I discovered there was that *it's all rigged in your favor.* There is a master sheet with everything on it. The angels and God Himself are all playing off that sheet, and it is the Word of God.

God's Word is ultimate and absolute. What He has said about you in Heaven is the absolute truth, and that is what you will be judged by. You will not be judged by what the devil tells you or what your friends tell you. The circumstances in your life do not dictate who you are. You are written in Heaven as being a specific person and doing the works of God through His Holy Spirit on this earth. Those are all written. There is no need for you ever to fail. You can win, but you have to learn how to stay in the Spirit.

Certain things have happened to you that are hindering you. You must deal with your hurts and forgive, forget, and let go of those things. It is not easy, but you have to do it for yourself. God gave us forgiveness for ourselves. Let Him deal with the people and you deal with the hurt that you have gone through. Do not let those people who did wrong have an advantage over you. If you do not forgive, then you become like they are. The reason that they are the way they are is that they have been hurt and are not walking in forgiveness. They have decided to be wrong and evil instead of doing what is right and good.

You do not want to become someone who hurts others and does wrong, but you can become like that if you get offended. You have to let offenses fall and forgive. Walk away from it and do not carry it with you. Then, let God heal you of those pathways that hurt. Trauma is not pleasant, but God can break the back of trauma in one single word.

> *I break trauma, and I drive those devils out. They are influencing you in the wrong way because they're taking advantage of your hurt. So right now, I drive you out, satan.*

And Father, with Your healing hand, right now touch the
people and heal them of their trauma, of all those hurts.

Right now, forgive anyone who has wronged you. Just do it. Say, "Father, I forgive them, and I release them. The cases are in Your hands now." Release those individuals into the hands of God and let Him take care of it. God is taking your hand and bringing you back, and that pathway is bright and glorious.

Imagine again that you are in eternity. You will see that everything works out; you are going to be with the heavenly Father by the river of life. You will be with Jesus, in the throne room. You are going to be eating from the trees and listening to the flowers sing, and it is just beautiful there. Everything is amazing. You are going to get to meet all the different people you have read about in the Bible. You are going to get to see your loved ones and everything is going to be okay.

So, you can get into that environment in your heart and your mind and then begin working backward, toward right now. First, you go to your future and frame your world by what the Word of God says. You realize that you are free and that you need to let go of trauma. Let God shine on that and then start to live your life. You know that God is shining a light on you to help you to deal with your hurt, and you are healed. As a result, you will turn and start ministering to people in the power of the Holy Spirit.

Once you have overcome this, you are going to be a powerhouse. You are going to lay hands on the sick. You will rebuke devils and they're going to scream and fly out of people. All of this will begin because you have allowed your heart to receive healing. You have not allowed those devils to influence you.

Remember that God is shining His spotlight on your heart because He wants to help you. And this is a time when you want the power of the Holy Spirit to heal you so that you can minister to others, which is the ultimate goal. God wants everyone healed. He wants every person walking in this. You can have victory in this life. You can live in the everlasting life that you're going to obtain in Heaven. You can live in that now. There is a way to do it. It involves tapping into what is in your heart. Your heart needs to receive healing. You are no longer a victim!

Chapter 13

The Foreknowledge
of the Almighty

*You perceive every movement of my heart
and my soul, and you understand my every
thought before even it even enters my mind.*

—Psalm 139:2 TPT

God knows and understands so much, and we understand so little because we are fallen. Through Jesus Christ, we have been redeemed from the curse—from death, hell, and the grave. There is a part of us that still needs to be awakened to the mysteries of God. There are things that Adam and Eve knew that we do not understand, and there are things that Jesus bought for us that we are still discovering.

You are diligent in studying and meditating on the Word of God, but the foreknowledge of God is so essential to understand. There is a part of God—His very personality—that we do not understand because of our perspective down here. However, if you were able to be where I was and see what I saw, you would not worry another day.

At times I catch myself worrying and becoming concerned because I get wrapped up in this realm and forget that there is an eternal realm where God has everything in control. Nobody is worried in Heaven, and there is no lack. Everybody is happy, and that is the way it should be down here, but it is not. So, if you are going to live successfully in this life, if you are going to walk in the Spirit and not fulfill the lusts of the flesh, you have to understand God's foreknowledge. You need to understand the different parts of you. Certain parts of you can pick up on God's foreknowledge, and there are certain parts of you, namely the soul and the body, that are not going to participate.

> *But he who is spiritual judges all things, yet he himself is rightly judged by no one* (1 Corinthians 2:15).

A carnal person is not going to be able to judge a spiritual person in any way; they are unable. A carnal person has no concept of what it is like to be spiritual. It is as though you know nothing about a car and a mechanic comes and tells you, "Okay well, this is what needs to be done to fix your vehicle." Now, even though you don't have any knowledge about cars, you still end up saying, "I'm not going to do that, that is not what needs to be done," and you give all your opinions. You do understand, but you are acting as though you do, and that is foolish.

There is a foolishness that comes from pride, and there is foolishness that comes from your lack of yielding. You have to learn how to yield and be humble and know that God knows a whole lot more than you, and He wants to tell you those things.

> *For what man knows the things of a man except the spirit of the man which is in him? Even so no one knows the things of God except the Spirit of God* (1 Corinthians 2:11).

Paul said that these things are mysteries, but the Spirit searches those mysteries and the deep things of God. However, God has revealed them to us through His Spirit. *"For the Spirit searches all things, yes, the deep things of God"* (1 Cor. 2:10). He said that God is the one who reveals, so He is going to reveal these deep things through Jesus Christ. All through his writings, Paul is unveiling these wonderful secrets that have been under the veil for so many years. These mysteries were even hidden from some of the prophets of old. They did not even know the things that we know now, by the Spirit of God. He has revealed these things to us.

MOVEMENT IN THE SPIRIT AND THE SOUL

Our scripture in Psalms says, *"You perceive every movement of my heart and my soul, and you understand my every thought before even it even enters my mind"* (Ps. 139:2 TPT). Wow! Did you hear what was just said? God already knows what we are going to say. He knows our thoughts. It is completely rigged in your favor if you will side with God!

The movement here is between your soul and your heart. There are movements in both according to Scripture. In First Thessalonians 5:23, Paul refers to our *"whole spirit, soul, and body."* We all have three parts. One is spiritual, one is psychological, and one is physical. Your body is physical, and your soul is the psychological part of you (the mind, will, and emotions), and there is your spirit-being. You have the flesh, which is your body, and that is your earth-suit, and it is where your spirit can contact this realm.

Your soul and spirit connect in the flesh so that you can experience different emotions, which helps you to be able to make choices. Your soul is making a connection with the body, which is your earth-suit. Your body is the one that contacts the physical realm, and your spirit is the real you that lives forever.

You are going to live forever. Whoever you are as a person continues to live forever, and not one person should ever have to go to hell. Jesus already bought them, but because they did not acknowledge Him they were never born again. Jesus said you cannot inherit the Kingdom of God unless you are born again (see John 3:3). Your spirit has to be changed by the recreation of the Spirit of God. Once that is accomplished, your body will need to be told what to do. Paul said, *"But I discipline my body and bring it into subjection, lest, when I have preached to others, I myself should become disqualified"* (1 Cor. 9:27).

He said that his body could disqualify him from the race. Paul also talked about the fact that his mind needed to be transformed (see Rom. 12:2). He spoke of being transformed by the renewing of the mind. Your mind has to be transformed by the Word of God. The Word of God will convince your mind of the way that it should go, and within the framework that you should think, and then your body will follow. You must get your spirit right by being born again, and then you build yourself up in the most holy faith by praying in the Holy Spirit.

You renew your mind by the Word of God so that your soul starts to side with your spirit. Then you tell your body, "This is the way it is going to be," and you start telling your body, "No, we are not going to do this." When you get all three to work together again, then this is the way it was before the fall. All three parts of you used to be in unity and works together. When Adam and Eve sinned the parts split, and now they fight each other.

Paul devotes an entire chapter of Romans to discussing a struggle within himself. He said that in his heart he wanted to do good, but he could not do it. We can see Paul's heart in his description of the war within (see Rom. 7).

Christians should be living in Romans 8, where it says that we are more than conquerors through Him who loved us. We have the power that raised Jesus from the dead dwelling in us. We can walk in the Spirit and overcome the power of the flesh. Most Christians, when you listen to them talk, they are living in Romans 7, which is Paul talking about how he was under the law, just trying to obey the rules, and he was not able to. Why? Because he said he did not have the power to see—the power came in the born-again experience—and that power came on the day of Pentecost through the baptism of the Holy Spirit.

The Holy Spirit within us, Christ the hope of glory, overcomes the mind and overcomes the flesh so that we walk in victory. God's foreknowledge is in your spirit. God is Spirit and, *"Those who worship Him must worship in spirit and truth"* (John 4:24). When you pray in the Spirit, you are building yourself up in the Holy Spirit, but you are also building yourself up in your spirit.

Paul says, *"For if you have the ability to speak in tongues, you will be talking only to God, since people won't be able to understand you. You will be speaking by the power of the Spirit, but it will all be mysterious"* (1 Cor. 14:2 NLT). He explains that your mind does not comprehend the psychological part of you that cannot participate in spiritual things. You have to yield to the Spirit in order to participate.

God's foreknowledge is a spiritual thing. He sees far ahead, and He hears, and He knows. God is a Spirit, so He is going to communicate to you through the Spirit. He is not going to talk to your mind because He is not a mind; He is a Spirit. He is not going to talk to you through your body because He is not a body; He is a Spirit. God is Spirit and His voice is deep within your heart telling you what to do. It is a spiritual thing. In God's foreknowledge, what He knows about your future is in the Spirit. The Holy Spirit was told to come. Jesus told His followers that He was leaving and sending back the Spirit of God to remind us of things that Jesus had said.

Jesus said the Holy Spirit will not talk on His own accord. He will only speak what the Father tells Him to. "He is going to remind you of the things that I have said, and He is going to reveal to you the future. He is going to tell you things to come" (see John 16:13). He is the Spirit of truth, and He is going to lead you into all truth.

CHOOSING GOOD

Jesus already set it up. He rigged it in your favor so that now you have the Holy Spirit inside of you and the Holy Spirit upon you. Those two things are working for you. However, your mind needs to come in line with God's Word and it must be transformed and renewed to do what the Spirit wants it to do. Then, as Paul said, the body has to be disciplined. Paul had to discipline his body so that after preaching Christ—being in the ministry—he would not be a castaway.

Paul is admitting that if he let himself be ruled by his body, then he could lose out. That doesn't seem right, but that is what the body does. The body wants to be connected to this realm and seek satisfaction in every area. That kind of satisfaction is selfish because it is not thinking of other people. When you walk in love, you are not going to do the things that your body wants to do because you are thinking of other people and their needs.

When you let your body rule, you start hurting other people. God's foreknowledge knows that you cannot go around doing what you want to do to fulfill your desires because you are going to be influencing and hurting someone else. We do not want to do that. We want to walk in love and that is why we walk in the Spirit and do not fulfill the lusts of the flesh.

In our verse, the psalmist says, *"You know every movement of my heart and every movement of my soul."* These are two different things. Because God knows this, the verse does not just stop there. It says, *"And you understand my every thought before it enters my mind."* Even the next thought that you are about to have, God already knows it. He does not stop you from doing wrong. He will let you do what is wrong. You can go and do wrong right now, and you can override what is right because you have a will. You have a soul, and that soul has a mind, will, and emotions, and you can decide what is right to do.

You discern between right and wrong, but you choose wrong. That is what happened with Adam and Eve when they ate of the fruit. They were able to know the difference between good and evil, and they chose evil. They could not handle being able to see and understand the difference between good and evil. You see, there was an age of innocence when Adam and Eve did not need to know evil because they were walking with God and created in His image. Only God can handle the ability to know good and evil and still choose good.

Remember that every day is filled with choices. There are decisions that you have to make that are going to influence your future, and they are going to influence the future of other people. That is why we need to walk in the Spirit and why we need to walk in love.

God is love—the very epitome of love. Love and God are the same and there is no difference. But always remember that love has everything to do with discipline as well. In Hebrews, God tells us that He disciplines those He loves.

> *For the Lord's training of your life is the evidence of his faithful love. And when he draws you to himself, it proves you are his delightful child* (Hebrews 12:6 TPT).

POSITION YOURSELF TO HEAR HIM

He is treating you as a son by disciplining you, and you know that. It is time to settle into walking in the Spirit. Let the Holy Spirit begin to produce the fruit in you. You can overcome the enemy and you can overcome everything in your life that is working against you if you will just trust in Him. Trust in God right now and allow Him to teach you and to tell you what it is that you need to do. It is based on what He already knows about you. God is not going to offer that information to you if you are not willing or wanting to know it. God knows when you are placing yourself in a position to hear and respect Him. What I have noticed about Jesus is that if you do not honor and respect Him for who He is, and if you do not discern who He is, you are going to walk away empty-handed. God wants you to discern who He is. He wants you to honor Him because He knows everything.

When I was with Him and talking to Him, I realized that there was nobody to appeal to besides Him because He was the advocate, or the intermediary, between God and man. He is the person you go to and say, "This is what I need." In reply, He says, "You can ask the Father and mention My name, and the Father is going to give it to you." Jesus' name is the password. Without Him, you can do nothing, but when you mention His name, you have access to God's foreknowledge, which means *it's all rigged.*

It is already set up for you, but you have to walk in it every day, and He is going to tell you to do things that might not go with your understanding. You may fight it in your mind because it seems like it does not make sense. God may take you in a direction that is opposite of where you are going. He might tell you something that is taking you in a different direction, but it is because He has foreknowledge and He knows exactly what He is doing.

Tap into this, because the Spirit of the Lord is always willing at any one moment to help you. The Lord has sent Him. He is your Helper and Advocate. The Holy Spirit's sole goal and assignment down here is to help you and to empower you to create an atmosphere where you can do what God is asking you to do. The Holy Spirit helps you to be successful and not just to be obedient. You can be willing and enjoy what God is doing in your life.

Here is the biggest thing to remember—when I was in Heaven, I saw that everything about our life is going to influence others whether we like it or not. The decisions you make today influence other people. Think about this—I saw that there were people I was destined to meet. I got to see the first 12 people I was going to be sent back for. I met all those people, and it took years. I think that I met the last one 20 years after they had been shown to me in Heaven. It was amazing to me that these people did not know me. They did not know it, but they were depending on me to be faithful. Not only to be sent back but then to walk this life out and then run into them one day because the angels were ushering me, showing me, and leading me to these people over the years.

It was amazing to me that when I spoke to them, the power of that other realm hit them. Each one began to weep under the power of God and destiny, and it was like a blanket around them. It just started to envelop them, and as they wept I saw that because I had been obedient and willing, the path that God had chosen for me with foreknowledge brought me to the right spot. I started to see people's lives changed, and that is the ultimate goal of a Christian. We are to change lives and go and help people and to preach the Gospel to the world.

How are we going to do that if we are not willing and obedient to walk in the Spirit and to yield to God's foreknowledge? If we do not honor, respect, and worship Jesus and know that He has our answers, then we are going to go away empty-handed. We have our own will, and that will can get us out of God's perfect will. It could move us out to where we think we know better and we can miss out totally.

I am telling you the truth, and I saw this when I was in Heaven. It is up to you to what degree or how close you want to walk with God. It truly is up to you, and you can choose not to walk with Him at all; it is your choice. However, if you decide to do less than one hundred percent, or nothing at all, that decision influences many people and can even influence other generations. Can you imagine being responsible for someone who lives in the next generation? You could be responsible for them. You did not discern that God is looking at an entirely bigger picture than you are. Generation after generation He is strategically setting it up because He has a goal in mind.

CALLED FOR THE GENERATIONS

If you are faithful in this generation, then you influence the next generation. Think about this—this book will be printed for years and years after I am gone. It will still be preaching and influencing lives even when I am gone. Think about the fact that you read about the apostle Paul in the Bible and everything he said is still influencing lives every day. He has been gone for two thousand years, and he is in Heaven in his mansion, right now, enjoying Heaven. His writings from a jail cell are still being read all over the world, and everybody's life is being changed by it.

He knows right now that we are talking about him. Paul the apostle knows that he is being spoken of and that his Gospel is being preached all over the world. He is so excited that he stayed faithful because it influenced generations to come. I know that you want to do that for God. I know that you want to count. Part of that is knowing that what is written about you in Heaven is foreknowledge. What God has written for a whole generation has to do with you doing your part, which has been written down in your book. Doing your part influences an entire generation, which then, in turn, influences the next generation.

Here is another mind-blowing revelation. I saw that we, in this generation, are actually answering the prayers of the previous generation. We are the answers to their prayers. When we were born, God had people pray. We find ourselves doing certain things, and we do not know why, but it is because somebody prayed and asked and believed God. We are fulfilling that desire because God remembers that generation.

When I saw these people when I was in Heaven and I met them on the earth, they were touched, and they were so thankful that I had spoken into their life. What was more important to me was that I saw the heart of God for those people. My life was rerouted, and I was sent back to speak. It just touches my heart to see how much God loves people.

I thought about this when I was asked if I wanted to come back. I said, "Lord, You know I want to be here with You. I want to go to Heaven." He told me that if I go back, I cannot fail. He said I would succeed, and I will see many people's lives changed and rerouted onto the correct path. He said, "If you do this, you will speak to them and cause them to understand and then walk correctly and walk into the perfect will of God."

I took God up on it because He said I could not fail. It is *all rigged in my favor*, and it is all rigged in your favor because God promised me that He would be with me and that I could not fail. Angels are on standby all the time to make sure that what God says happens in your life.

The Holy Spirit lives in my spirit; He is part of the Trinity. He already knows my next move because the Holy Spirit is inside of me, so He is touching my spirit right now. He is influencing me. My next step is already known inside of me. Inside of you right now, there is a place where God is revealing to you, in your very inner part, the next step.

Even though your head does not comprehend it, you can feel joyful inside and be sad in your emotions. You can be sick in your body and be happy and feeling like dancing in your spirit. That is because God is in there, and He is speaking your future, and it is time for us to allow that understanding of the Holy Spirit to communicate to our mind. It is time to let the plan and the purposes of God be revealed in our lives and let the Holy Spirit do His work.

THE GREATER WALK

Initially, we all think that because we are born again, now we are not going to hell and we are going to go to Heaven and everybody is excited about that. We are now starting to find out that there is a deeper walk with Jesus while we are here. We are not just hiding out until the end comes; instead, we are supposed to be down here ruling and reigning and taking dominion over all the territory that satan has stolen from us.

We need to get it back for God, and we do that by driving out the devil, preaching the Gospel, and dispelling the wrong ideas. We do it by taking the limitations off of people and beginning to speak from people's futures. That is why prophecy, words of knowledge, and words of wisdom are such ultimate tools. When you speak prophetically and speak words about people's futures, and when you speak words of knowledge that pinpoint what people are going through, you are giving them answers. The Holy Spirit of God is confirming the covenant that God gave us as His children.

Even though God can go to our future, He can come to our now and talk to us, and it seems profound because He uses men and women of God to speak to us. It is prophetic. He is there talking from your future, and men and women are telling you this is what God has planned for you, and it encourages you.

The ultimate goal of a prophet is to speak so that they get people to start walking in it. To begin walking in their future, allowing God to form the thought processes and to accept an idea so that you are ready to accept your future.

Are you ready to start thinking above and beyond what you have been able to by allowing God to give you things in your spirit? God wants to give you things exceedingly above and beyond what you could ask or think. Are you ready to encounter the same Jesus I did when He said, "Kevin, if you will believe, nothing shall be impossible to you." When He said nothing, He meant nothing. There was no way that I could be denied if I grasped this and had faith in my heart and trusted in Him. There was no way that I would be denied.

How would you like that? How would you like to grasp ahold of your future right now and refuse to let go of it until you pull it into your now? Well, that is possible, and that is what prayer is. Jesus showed me that He is standing in our future, and He is bidding us to come to Him. He is asking us to come to Him right now and walk into our future. In the Spirit, there is no distance, and there is no time.

You need to be encouraged. God is with you in a powerful way, and there is no way that He is going to let you fail. He wants to be in there with you. We need to yield to Him and give our will over to Him. Are you ready for that? Are you ready to grasp the realities of the future because God is handing them to you through Jesus Christ right now by the Spirit?

Right now, you can receive:

> *Father, in the name of Jesus, I break every power against the people that is keeping them from receiving right now. Father, by Your Spirit, minister the reality of their future to them in the name of Jesus. I thank You, Holy Spirit, that You will go right in there and bring up the realities. Release people right now into their future. Show them how good it is and how good You are. Thank You, Father. I release people right now into Your perfect will. "No good thing will I withhold from those who love Me and fear Me and walk according to My statutes," says the Lord. "I am with those who love Me, I am the high and lofty one, but I also dwell with the humble and contrite in spirit, and no good thing am I going to withhold from those people."*

That is what the Lord says, and right now He is ministering to you under the power of love. Right now, God loves you, and He is concerned about you. Nothing is impossible if you will believe. The Spirit of God is still ministering to people, and many people right now are being healed and set free. God is setting you free in the name of Jesus. Just release your past; God is in your future. Walk with Him right now. It is going to be okay; God is with you. He is with you in a mighty way, walking with you in the name of Jesus.

Chapter 14

YOU ARE CHOSEN

*This is just too wonderful, deep, and
incomprehensible! Your understanding of
me brings me wonder and strength.*
—PSALM 139:6 TPT

IT IS EXCITING WHAT PSALM 139 IS BRINGING FORTH.
God is saying amazing things that we did know about, but
by His Spirit He is revealing secrets today. It is lovely how
all of these truths were here in Psalm 139, but I had never
seen them. When the Spirit of God was able to open my
eyes and my understanding, then all these things came out.
When I was in Heaven with Jesus, He showed me step by
step these things in all the Scriptures.

I want to share this with you; in Psalm 139:6 it says,
*"This is just too wonderful, deep, and incomprehensible!
Your understanding of me brings me wonder and strength"*

(TPT). There is this idea that God has chosen us. Paul talked about this when he said that all the good works that we were predestined to do in Christ were already wrapped up in the work of Jesus Christ:

> *For we are God's masterpiece. He has created us anew in Christ Jesus, so we can do the good things he planned for us long ago* (Ephesians 2:10 NLT).

PREDESTINED FOR HEAVEN

I always wondered about predestination; how much should we play into that? I was brought up in a church that taught that if you were going to hell, it was already predestined. I was told that you could not even witness to these people because they were destined for hell and that there were only certain people who were chosen to go to Heaven. Then I visited Heaven, and Jesus explained the Scriptures in an even more significant measure.

When I came back, I started to study a lot. When I was studying, I found out that predestination is not what we thought. We know that we cannot make people do things. God does not either. He gives us free will to do what we choose. He offers what He has for us and He provides the best, and that is all He does. He helps us to know the truth by the Spirit of God. The truth will set you free. Jesus said that the Spirit of truth will lead you into all truth. The Spirit will set you free: *"For the Lord is the Spirit, and wherever the Spirit of the Lord is, there is freedom"* (2 Cor. 3:17 NLT).

> *Therefore if the Son makes you free, you shall be free indeed* (John 8:36).

We encounter this freedom because the Spirit of God leads you into truth, and then that truth sets us free. The revelation of the Spirit of God is of utmost importance. He brings us revelation. When I was in Heaven with Jesus, I saw that God predestined everyone to be in Heaven. It is people who choose not to go.

It was a profound truth to me when I realized that people should not even be in hell. Jesus told me that hell was made for the devil and his angels; it was not prepared for man. Man was not supposed to go to hell, but it is because they reject what Jesus has done for them.

Paul discusses this in Second Corinthians 5. The entire chapter focuses on the *ministry of reconciliation.* It follows what I was also taught by Jesus in Heaven—that God already has a plan, and *it's all rigged* in everyone's favor through Jesus Christ. He was the Lamb who was slain before the foundations of the world. Jesus planned to come back and buy back humanity before man had even been created and placed in the Garden.

MERCY IN HIS FOREKNOWLEDGE

Again, the psalmist says, "It's just too wonderful and deep and incomprehensible." The Trinity determined, long before man came on the scene, that Jesus would come and die and redeem humankind. Before creation, God already in His foreknowledge knew that we would fall. God did not prevent it because He cannot override our will. As a provision for us, He made a way of escape. God made a way for redemption, and He saw this way ahead of time. Jesus was that Lamb who was slain from the foundation of the world (see Rev. 13:8).

Paul told us that we are predestined to do these certain works in Christ Jesus. That was the package that was made—the salvation package. Not only was it planned for Jesus to redeem us, but then it was planned for Him to give us gifts of the Spirit as an enablement for us to be gifts to this world and the Body of Christ.

If we choose to be born again and walk according to the Lord, then all these beautiful things are going to happen that have been written for us. If not, then we are going to be used by evil spirits. People who are not saved, as well as Christians and anyone who does not submit to God, enable evil spirits to come in and influence them.

People in the world who are not born again have no way of withstanding that power of satan, and as a result they will do his bidding, and they have no way of stopping that. Christians, on the other hand, can resist him. They can submit to God, resist the devil, and he will flee from them (see James 4:7). Jesus said that *"Many are called, but few are chosen"* (Matt. 22:14), and very narrow is the way that leads to everlasting life, but very wide is the way that leads to destruction (see Matt. 7:13-14). There is often resistance to the truths that I am teaching. When you go to Heaven, it changes your thinking and your perception. It is not always easy to grasp these truths, but I must continue to teach them to people.

MINISTRY OF RECONCILIATION

Paul teaches about the ministry of reconciliation in Second Corinthians 5. He explains that the price has been paid and that you have been reconciled with God through Jesus Christ. Accept Jesus Christ and His work on the cross, and then make Him your Lord and Savior. Confess Him as Lord, and you will receive salvation and then you will be born again and go to Heaven. Before you go there, you will walk in a life that is powerful, where you display the glory of God.

We must be careful about how we portray God's will. Christians sometimes do not give God the glory. God wishes that everyone would prosper and be in good health even as their soul prospers (see

3 John 1:2). That is the Word of God. We have to start to correct our thinking and not allow our experience and what we have seen and heard to affect us. We need to think and speak according to what God says in His Word that speaks to us from the other realm.

Paul says, *"We make it our passion to persuade others to turn to Him"* (2 Cor. 5:11 TPT). And He goes on to speak of the reconciliation, where God is not angry at their sin anymore. Jesus met the requirement for us by purchasing humanity through His blood. Once you accept that, your role is to announce it for other people to accept it. If they do not accept it, they go to hell—a place that no man is supposed to go.

In Heaven, I saw that we are chosen and God wrote it as though everyone would come to Heaven because He wanted His family back. He did not destine anybody to go to hell. When we fell, He had to purchase us back. Because of this world and the deception of the devil, people will not accept the truth. It is very hard down here sometimes to get people to accept the truth and even more so with Christians who have been wrongly educated and informed. They are holding on to things that limit them. It's not the truth. God has not spoken that, and they repeat it as though it is the Word of God.

What they speak is not the Word of God because the counsel of God is the whole Bible, and everything in it has been placed together. Your belief system is based on many Scriptures, not just on one. You can look into it and see the personality of God. You see His ways and get to know Him. It is not based on just one Scripture that you wave around. Doctrine is based on many Scriptures and the character of God that is revealed through Scripture.

You are chosen, but you were chosen for life. You were chosen to prosper, chosen to be healthy, and chosen to win, yet this world is fallen, and things break. Difficulties happen, and it is a struggle sometimes, as there is a war that goes on. However, that does not change the fact that you are chosen. That does not change the fact that the understanding of God coming into your life brings you strength, and it causes you to realize that God chose you in Christ before the foundations of the world. He chose you to be redeemed. That is not predestination in the sense that some are going to go to hell and some people are going to go to Heaven, and you have been predestined to be a Christian. No! God bought back humanity through Jesus Christ. Period.

The ministry of reconciliation must be preached. We go out and proclaim the Good News, and we heal the sick. We raise the dead, we speak in tongues, and we drive out devils. We do all of that because that is the Kingdom of God advancing. What is it that you are chosen to do? Why is it that you even ask these questions? Well, you are asking these questions because you are hungry inside. You want to know that you are special and that there is a plan and a purpose for you. There is a plan and a purpose for you, and His plan and purpose for you is beyond what your mind can even comprehend.

You Have Been Chosen

You have been chosen. There are specific things that are written about you, and God has gone to your future. He is standing in your future right now. He has equipped you to walk in your future now. God wants you to be successful in this life and do what you have been called to do. It is discovery, and it is a journey that is being revealed and unveiled by the Spirit of God. The Spirit of God is your friend, and He is the one who is going to come alongside you and be an Advocate and a Helper. He is going to be a Counselor to you, and He is going to speak to you and engage you and cause you to walk in the truth.

When God chooses someone, He also provides for them, and God is not going to let you go. There is a plan and a purpose. *"And we know that all things work together for good to those who love God, to those who are the called according to His purpose"* (Rom. 8:28). It is all working toward your favor and toward your good. He can change and reroute things so that you never really lose. No matter what happens today, God can reverse it tomorrow; God can change things. There are all kinds of things that He can do. Your goal every day should be to seek God and find out what He is saying. You can do this by framing your world with the Word of God. You study the Word, and in small amounts you meditate and think about these things and let them become part of you.

It is not enough that you can recite Scripture. You have to be able to understand Scripture to where it is implemented in your life and it becomes a way of life—a truth that you live by. When you sense the Spirit of God moving on you, you can move with Him and be empowered by Him. You are not empowered by knowledge alone but by understanding what God has chosen you to do. There are all these things listed in each one of our books. Angels read these books and they are sent and assigned to us, and they are going to implement what is in your book if you are willing. You must have the revelation that God has chosen you.

The power of the Holy Spirit is ministering to people right now. There are many reading this, and you feel that because of what has happened in your life you were not chosen and are not special. God is saying, "The enemy did not want you to succeed. He does not want you to come into the call that you have been chosen to do, because you are such a threat to him; satan is afraid of you." He is afraid that if you get too much momentum into what God has called you to do, you will be empowered beyond what he could stop. So he has to slow you down and get you into fear. He has to get you into the unknown where you are unsure.

But here is the thing—your "knower," which is inside of you, is your spirit and the Holy Spirit together. Revelation does not just come up into your understanding, because we live in this fallen world. It is so hard to be in this realm after being in the heavenly realm because nothing seems to work perfectly down here. Nobody is perfect down here. So even when God does speak, there may be eight different opinions about what He just said. It is just like when you tell somebody something and three minutes later they are asking you what you said. You could tell people things three times, and they still do the opposite of what you said. Well, that is because it is a fallen world. Why is it that your garage or bedroom does not straighten up by itself? Everything goes to chaos because it is a fallen world, and it works the opposite of what we are made to be.

We are made to have excellence and be perfect. We are just like God, as He has made us in His image according to Genesis 1:26. And the power that raised Jesus from the dead is bringing us back into that walk in the Spirit. We have to start to realize that the way God made us was because He chose us. Because He chose us, nothing can come against us.

> So now I live with the confidence that there is nothing in the universe with the power to separate us from God's love. I'm convinced that his love will triumph over death, life's troubles, fallen angels, or dark rulers in the heavens. There is nothing in our present or future circumstances that can weaken his love. There is no power above us or beneath us—no power that could ever be found in the universe that can distance us from God's passionate love,

which is lavished upon us through our Lord Jesus, the
Anointed One! (Romans 8:38-39 TPT)

SPEAK WHERE YOU ARE GOING

God is working His purpose in your life, and you need to be encouraged. Do not let other people discourage you. I do not even listen to people when they start to speak the devil's words. There is a certain point where you know you are done because you only want to hear words of life. So if a person cannot do something for me that God has asked me to do, then I am going to find somebody who can. If you cannot do something that you need to, go and find someone who can. The Lord has taught me that you could do this, but if you find yourself in a situation where you cannot, then you need to find someone to help you who is able. The Body of Christ fulfills each other's needs.

You are supposed to have other people in your life who are on the same page with you and are on the same page as the Word of God. God always honors His Word and He recognizes His Word when it is being spoken. If you are chosen, then you are going to be on the same page as God, if you so choose. After that, anyone who comes into your life is chosen, and they are going to be on the same page as you.

If people are not speaking the direction that you are going, and if you are not speaking where you are going, then you are in trouble because your tongue is a rudder according to the Book of James. Whatever you speak determines the direction that you are heading (see James 3:4). That is why Jesus said if you have a mountain in your way and you want it to get out of the way, then you speak to it. You believe in your heart that what you say with your mouth is going to happen, and it shall be done whenever you pray (see Mark 11:23). He said that you should believe that you receive what you just prayed when it has not even manifested yet. You are fully convinced because faith is of the heart; it is not of the head. You do not have faith in your body; you have faith in your heart.

So do not listen to people who are hindering you. Stop looking at things and listening to things that are not taking you where you need to go. Certain things are not going to fulfill your future. God has chosen you for a specific mission and specific task. He has made you the way you are for a certain reason because He has a plan. The angels understand this and all the saints who have gone to Heaven understand. All the patriarchs and prophets understand all this, and they just believe that you are going to get it. You can see that you have been chosen in this generation to change this generation and to reroute people into the path of righteousness and justice so that you can experience what God has for you and you can help others to do the same.

It is amazing to me that God is seated on a throne, and the foundation of His throne are layers of righteousness and justice. Truth and faithfulness are in His throne (see Ps. 89). God is based on truth, justice, and righteousness. So when He speaks, He speaks from that platform. When He spoke about your life, it was already complete and it is going to happen, because what the Lord sends out by His Word does not come back void.

> So shall My word be that goes forth from My mouth; it shall not return to Me void, but it shall accomplish what I please, and it shall prosper in the thing for which I sent it (Isaiah 55:11).

Do not doubt God's Word or downplay His Word. It should be the most important thing in your life. Thus, the profound truth in the Scripture is that God has already planned things out. And when

He planned these things out, He already knew that there would be people who were going to resist you. He already knew there were things that were going to break and that would not work out.

God already knew all this. He knew that your job was going to disappear and that you would need another one. He knew that your car was going to wear out and you would need another one. He understood all that, and yet He is not concerned. He wants to provide for you. Well, how is God going to provide for you? He prepares His provision ahead of time; it is all stored up. I saw this is Heaven—there is nothing that catches God by surprise. What aspect of life is worrying you? First Peter 5:7 says, *"Casting all your care upon Him, for He cares for you."*

There is a process of you building your faith and trust in God through praying in the Spirit and meditating on the Word of God. It happens through communication and fellowship in the Holy Spirit. You must learn to turn your will over to Him, crucifying the flesh and walking in the Spirit. Jesus said that you have to deny yourself and pick up your cross if you want to follow Him (see Luke 14:27).

It is amazing that the Gospel does not have to change. The same message that was good enough with Jesus is good enough for now. There is no difference. It is the same God and the same truth. When I met Jesus, He spoke the Bible the whole time I was with Him. Every time He has appeared to me, He has spoken Scripture. He has already chosen a certain way to do things, and He has a certain path. He has an intent for the ages. He is not worried or behind in any way. We are the ones who are behind and who are holding things back. It is because we are fallen. God has redeemed our fallen nature through Jesus Christ. It would be best if you allowed those benefits to come forth so that you can see them.

I think that most of us need to know what comes with our purchase. If you are buying something, you like to know exactly what you get and what benefits come with what you purchased. You want to know how your life will be different and what needs your purchase will be fulfilling. When a consumer product is designed, the creator is aware of people's needs. God does this as well; He designs salvation to meet people's needs. He did not just make a bunch of rules for us to break to be able to point out how weak we are. God did not give us the law so that He can show off and tell us that we are losers. He did all of what He did because He knew what we needed, and He made provision for the need. Whatever it is you are going through in your life right now, trust in Him, knowing that He has chosen you and knows everything about you. It may be too incomprehensible for you, but you have to accept the fact that He has your answer and a solution for you. You do not have anything to worry about! I know it is not easy to get out of your mind.

The Spirit of the Lord is telling me that there are many books that need to be written in this realm. God wants many of you to write your testimony. God wants you to write about a particular area because people need to hear what you have to say. He is telling me that there is music that has to be brought into this realm that no one else is going to do. You have to put yourself in that place. God wants to use you to help people. Whatever it is that is in your heart, whatever it is that God is calling you to do, it is to meet a need. God wants to meet people's needs through you.

Right now, by the impartation of the Holy Spirit, I release your gifting to come forth. I see the Holy Spirit counseling every person who is reading these words. He is causing you to understand, and He is taking you by the hand and developing those gifts in you. God is showing you what your talents are. He is showing you which jobs to take and what route you should go on that will help to develop your gifts. He wants to get you to the place where you are an answer to someone's need. A place where you become God's provision for a person's needs. God is using you. Your market value has just increased because God is touching you and laying hands on you. There are many needs in the world, and God wants to meet those needs through you.

He is causing your value to go through the roof right now because you have something inside of you that everyone else needs. God is causing this to happen to many of you who are reading this book.

> *In Jesus' name, I release you! You are chosen of God, and He has a plan for your life. You do not need to doubt or fear anymore. I break the power of the enemy, and I drive out every evil spirit. I break your power; let go of God's people. I drive every evil spirit out right now in the name of Jesus. Thank You, Lord, for healing people's bodies right now and delivering them from all kinds of depression in Jesus' name. I break the power of satan over your life!*

Chapter 15

You Can Outlast the Devil

MY WIFE AND I WERE SITTING IN A CHINESE RESTAUrant with our spiritual parents, and as we ate my spiritual father, Jesse Duplantis, a well-known minister of the Gospel, preached to us for almost an hour on how you can outlast the devil. He proclaimed that the Lord told him—you can outlast the devil!

The Lord wants me to ignite you to understand where you are right now and that it's time for the "showdown." The funny thing about this is that you have no limitations, but the devil does have limitations. You have been taught your whole life, through the media and other voices, that if you strive you can do this or that. If you push and manipulate and get yourself in a secure position, you can promote yourself and you will succeed.

Jesus came and said, *"For whoever desires to save his life will lose it, but whoever loses his life for My sake will save it"*

(Luke 9:24). Everything about Jesus Christ was counterculture, and it does not always go over very well. The world promotes a certain system, but that system is set up for failure. No matter what you do, you cannot win, and it is already set up that way. You cannot pay off your loans, and it is mathematically set up so that no matter what you do you will never get ahead. You did not know it until now because now I am telling on the devil.

What Jesus came to do was to reconcile you to God and cancel your debt. However, you still spend the rest of your life in debt. Why? Because you live here, but you are not in debt in Heaven. No one in Heaven is limiting you, and right now everyone in the cloud of witnesses is cheering you on from Heaven. They have no doubt about what you are called to do and never doubt that you will completely fulfill it. But you must outlast the devil. The devil believes that he has you in checkmate and thinks that he has you in a corner. The devil thinks that he has it all rigged in his favor. The bottom line is that when Jesus came, He turned the tables on the devil.

The apostle Paul was the only one who had the inside scoop on what Jesus did. Paul was caught up to Heaven where he received his Gospel, and then he wrote letters to the churches. If it were not for him, we would know about Christ, but we would not know what we had *in* Christ. We would know how many loaves and fish there were and where Jesus went every day because it was all recorded. However, to understand our position in Christ, this came through Paul.

Paul knew what we had, and he was fiercely against those who came in to preach false doctrine and teach things that were not true. So the warfare that he went through as an apostle was to keep people on track. Paul pulled back the veil to show them what was behind it. The Corinthians were carnal, and Paul wanted to take a belt to them. However, the Corinthians considered themselves spiritual.

What was wrong was that they had not lived crucified lives. Paul had to forcefully come in and draw boundaries that they should have already known.

Jesus is the Apostle over our faith. He is the Supreme King over our faith, which means that He starts your faith and He finishes your faith. The bottom line is that there is nothing else after Him. When I met Jesus, I could not appeal beyond Him if I did not like what He was telling me. There is no suggestion box in Heaven. You have to agree with God in absolutely everything because there is no appeal past Jesus Christ. He is the one who started your faith, and He will finish in absolute truth.

The reason that people went on conquests and won in their walk of faith in Hebrews 11 was that they knew God. They saw "Him who is invisible." They were looking for a city whose builder and maker was God. They knew how to look into the spirit realm and see what was true, and then they implemented it in this realm. What I just told you will save your life and make you whole. Jesus said to me that He went through everything so that everyone will receive healing if they take part at the table. However, the enemy does not want you to come to the table, because at the table is everything you will ever need.

Paul had authority because he had seen Jesus Christ and said, *"From now on let no one trouble me, for I bear in my body the marks of the Lord Jesus"* (Gal. 6:17). Paul spent most of his life in jail for what he believed. Are you ready to do that? The cost is worth it.

The process that you have to go through is that you have to enter in through death. Everyone who came into the Promised Land had to go across the Jordan. Jesus had to be baptized to fulfill that same righteousness. He had to be baptized in the Jordan River because it represented death. Then through this death, you go into the Promised Land. Why are you waiting until you die to go to the Promised Land?

It is because the fight down here is difficult, and everybody gets into survival mode. Then they watch all their favorite prophecy teachers, which I love too, and after a few years of storing up baked beans and water, you think, "Maybe it's time for me to go out and be a witness. Maybe it's time to feed the poor and write some books and get on TV and tell the world about Jesus." I am not going to promote your survival mentality; that is not why I came back. I was sent back to break yokes and not to put them on you.

If every year the prophets are saying, "This is the year for breakthrough," but you are still taking pills, still depressed, still not healed, and still poor, then there is something wrong. God has a system, and He set in the church some to be apostles, prophets, pastors, teachers, and evangelists (see Eph. 4:11). These are set in the churches as the government of God. You cannot wake up in the morning and say "I am an apostle." You cannot go and print out your certificate online, sign it yourself, and now you are an apostle. That is not the way it works. Everyone I know who is an apostle or a prophet does not want to be one because the price is so high. I know prophets who are the most accurate on the earth, and they hide.

There is a prophet I know whom many other prophets call for a word from God. I will not call him for one, but I will call to give him a word. My reason for this is because he is a person too, and he needs to be with friends. When he calls me, he will spend five hours with me. While you are here on this earth, you are not supposed to be surviving; you are here to give out. You are here as the Body of Christ to build each other up. Even prophets and apostles need help; they need a word. They need you to be who you are. The Body of Christ is going to rise, and we can break the powers of the enemy right now.

As you can tell, I have an edge about me now because I am done playing around with the devil. There is a room that the devil wants to put you in, and it's called the drama room. When you are in that room, all of a sudden you start to feel your body. You begin to notice everything about yourself, your mind, your reactions, and you begin to feel like you do when you are watching the movie *Jurassic Park*. When you walked out of the *Jurassic Park* movie, you were looking for the T-rex and the raptor because that movie moved your sense of reality to the point where you felt it in your body. You watch movies like *The Bourne Identity*, and it seems like it is reality.

I have friends who are super soldiers, and many of these movie depictions are true. So when you walk out of one of those movies, you feel like you are being followed. You are thinking, "How am I going to change the clip in my pistol fast enough and turn and fire in all different directions the way he did in the movie?" In the meantime, you are only going to lunch, but you know the man taking your order is a double agent! What I am saying is that if a movie can shift your reality, satan can too.

You are not called to survive down here. You are called to thrive and rule as a king and a priest. Did you know that is what you are? When I was in Heaven, I saw all of this, and I'm not holding back anymore. Today is the day when I just let go, and I am emptying all my "clips." You will start seeing trends, and you realize that you are on to the devil. The devil, as a sniper, thinks that he can go around and that he will get his target. But little does he know that someone is following him, and it is me. I am following the devil. He has a small red dot on the back of his head, and it is from your gun. You see, you have to get him on the run because you are on to him and you know who you are in Christ Jesus.

When are we going to use our head and our spirit and just become spirit-filled human beings who walk in authority? The devil does not want you down here on earth, ruling, reigning, and thriving. The devil wants to wrap it up so that he can appear on the scene as the antichrist and take over. That is the summation of most end-time prophecy teachings. However, you should never go to the table of the Lord and just pick up end-time prophecy or deliverance off of it. You should eat *all* that God has provided for you and become balanced. There is a valid need for everything that God has on that table. I am not going to focus on one thing in my ministry because I have the ministry of Jesus.

When I was with Jesus, I asked Him why no one has ever said they want the mantle of Jesus. If you meet Him, there is no one in the whole existence of any universe that is as beautiful as He is. Why would I want to talk to the teller at the bank when I can speak to the president of the bank. If somebody tells me, "No," I find somebody who can tell me, "Yes." That is what my spiritual father Jesse Duplantis taught me. Jesse was checking into a five-star hotel, and his room was to be ready at three o'clock because he had prepaid. However, when he arrived, his room was not prepared, and it was now five o'clock. He told them that they had to do something quickly because he had already paid for the past two hours. He was told that his room was not clean and nothing could be done. He told them that if they could not do anything about it, then they needed to find somebody who could. Finally, he talked to the manager. He asked why it was that he had paid for the room two months before to be ready at three o'clock and it was now five o'clock and he was not in his room yet. They knew he was coming, and it was the biggest suite that they had. After that, they went right up and cleaned, and they gave him the suite for free.

When you are told, "No," you have to appeal to someone higher. Jesus already said, *"If you can believe, all things are possible to him who believes"* (Mark 9:23). What if you just went to the CEO of your faith, a Person who can say that if it is possible it will be done. Well, Jesus already said all things are possible to him who believes. Jesus said, *"Do you believe that I am able to do this?"* (Matt. 9:28).

> *And he fell on his face and implored Him, saying, "Lord if you are willing, You can make me clean. Then He put out His hand and touched him, saying, "I am willing; be cleansed"* (Luke 5:12-13).

What I want to reveal to you is that Jesus is much stronger in His personality than you have been taught.

ENTERING YOUR FUTURE

The Father, the Son, and the Holy Spirit are one, and you come to the Father in Jesus' name. Jesus is the end of your faith, and you must get acquainted with Him more deeply. When you go deeper with Christ, your life is going to get ignited. In order for your faith to come out as pure gold, you have to be tested in the fire. I am speaking to you, not as Kevin, but I am speaking to you from Jesus Himself. Jesus has taken over my body, and now it is as though He is living His life in and through me right now. That is what a true Christian is—Christ living through me. He is telling you that you need to release yourself into the Holy Fire; it is your entrance into your future. Everyone has to enter into the Holy Fire, and I know this from searching Scriptures for fifteen hours a day for many, many years.

I am going toward the mark: *"I press toward the goal for the prize of the upward call of God in Christ Jesus"* (Phil. 3:14). The reason that I am saying this is that I am finished with drama. Drama stalls you; it draws your attention away. People get caught up in their emotions, and they get out of the realm of the spirit where they can win; instead, they find themselves in a ring with the devil where he can beat them.

Do you want to be lit up and on fire and oppose satan? Do you want to be God's people called to promote the Kingdom of God on earth? If you are going to be in the army of God, advancing at an alarming rate, then you need to be set on fire and not resist the fire.

You need to live a holy life, and you cannot do it on your own. You have been bought with a price, and God owns you, and it is His job to clean you up with Holy Fire. The problem is that no one wants to submit to God for this to happen. When you preach on holiness, no one wants to give you a good offering because it is not popular. In fact, your large church will turn into seventeen people very quickly. No one wants to hear that you have to die in order to live, or that you must give to receive or that you have to lose to win. The devil thinks he has this whole culture locked up. The culture tells you to promote yourself, and if the glory does not show up, there are smoke machines and lights. It is ugly to God whenever you promote yourself; it stinks. However, *"Surrender yourselves to God to be his sacred, living sacrifices. And live in holiness, experiencing all that delights his heart"* (Rom. 12:1 TPT)—*"an offering and a sacrifice to God for a sweet-smelling aroma"* (Eph. 5:2).

Do you want the glory of God? If you want a move that never ends in your church, what you have to do is go to where the move is already happening and then come back with it. That is what the prophets of old and what all the generals of the faith did. They went to where it was happening, and they got it, and then they took it to a generation. With that being said, you have to be a carrier of the glory, and that is not so easy.

I am not talking about being a Christian or not being a Christian, and I am not talking about going to Heaven or not going to Heaven. I am asking, do you want to change history? The people who change history surrender themselves and pick up their cross, and they follow Jesus (see Matt. 16:24). Now when I do that, it costs me everything.

Once, a popular man of God pointed his finger at me, and said, "You are going to have my ministry, but it is going to cost you everything; you are going to die to self." That was in 1986, and I had already left everything, and I was trying to think of what else I could give up. I had no idea how much pride I had in me until after he laid hands on me and prophesied over me for 20 minutes. Since 1986, the Holy Spirit has been working on me until today, and now I stand under the authority of what he laid hands on me to do. Since 1986, that anointing has been working its way into me and it has been driving me out.

I wrote a book because the Lord asked me to. I did not wait because as soon as the Lord talks to me, I go and do it. He told me I was to write a book called *Holy Fire*. I started writing it three years ago. I have written many books since then, and I cannot get *Holy Fire* published because I have been in a fight with the devil over it. When I got halfway done writing it, the Holy Spirit spoke to me. I thought it was good, but He said that it was just like every other holy book that has ever been written. The Holy Spirit asked if I was ready to hear how He wanted it written, and He told me to write it from lucifer's perspective.

Every angel and every cherub has God's name, "El," somewhere in their name—Gabriel, Michael, Israel for examples. I asked God why lucifer's name did not have El in it when he was made perfect. What was his real name? The Holy Spirit gave me a Scripture, so I went directly to the Hebrew, which I can read. I looked, and it said, "heylel," which translated to lucifer. Why did the scholars hide the fact that lucifer's real name is heylel? The name heylel means "the bright and shining one of God," and it is apparent in Scripture. The name lucifer is just a Babylonian god's name.

"Thus says the Lord God: 'You were the seal of perfection, full of wisdom and perfect in beauty'" (Ezek. 28:12). There was no one higher in perfection; heylel knew holiness, and he walked in the midst of the fiery stones. I saw those stones in heaven, and I walked on them. They are blue stones of sapphire; they are on fire with the holiness of God. Jesus stopped me before I stepped onto them and said, "You did not ask Me." I responded and said, "I am the righteousness of God in Christ Jesus, set apart holy unto You." I was quoting all the faith scriptures that I had learned at college. Jesus told me that it was not about position but about relationship. Only those who walked in the fear of the Lord on the earth, as Enoch did, get to walk on these stones. I said, "This was not what I was taught. You bought my position." Jesus said, "This is not position; this is a privilege because you walked in the fear of the Lord; this is relationship." Then I realized the truth of the scripture:

> *Not everyone who says to Me, "Lord, Lord," shall enter the kingdom of heaven, but he who does the will of My Father in heaven. Many will say to Me in that day, "Lord, Lord, have we not prophesied in Your name, cast out demons in Your name, and done many wonders in Your name?" And then I will declare to them, "I never knew you; depart from Me, you who practice lawlessness!"* (Matthew 7:21-23)

They did not have relationship with Him, and this is a message that is not popular to preach because it offends people. Jesus said, "Welcome to My life, because that is the way it was for Me every day." The truth is, satan resists any revelation that exposes his inner workings and the original understanding of holiness as he once walked with God on the fiery stones (see Ezek. 28).

You have to be able to understand your enemy, and you have to get into his head. He becomes predictable because you get to know him. What would you do if you were the one who was out, and the enemy was in? How would you try to destroy him knowing that you cannot win? You see, satan cannot win and he knows that his only hope is to destroy you so that he can get to God that way. How would you come against the Christian if you were satan? How satan does it is that he causes Christians to think in terms of position and not a relationship with their heavenly Father. This position causes Christians to believe in extreme grace, and they believe that God loves them, and they can do whatever they want. On the day of judgment, they will find out that this was very wrong.

I was sent back to tell you this, but the problem we are having here is that no one wants to submit to the holy fire. You want everything. You want resurrection, but you do not want to die first, but you must die before you can be resurrected. *"Most assuredly, I say to you, unless a grain of wheat falls into the ground and dies, it remains alone; but if it dies, it produces much grain"* (John 12:24). This Scripture is God's order.

The Gospel of Jesus Christ is very simple. We have made it very hard with countless DVD sets and manuals. God is not complicated at all when you look at Him through His Spirit living inside of you. You have the equipment to go to the table and eat. We have made it something so complicated that we cannot even enter in ourselves. That sounds like what the Pharisees were doing in Jesus' day. Goats do not do anything that they are supposed to do, and they resist everything. They will not submit to authority; they are rebellious. If you go toward a goat, they will plant their feet. I know this to be true because I have done it. With lambs, they will let you pick them up, and you can lead them; you do not have to drive them. With goats, you are in for a ride if you grab their horns or do anything to try to tame them. The religious system and religious leaders of Jesus' day is what killed Him. They could not do it themselves, so they got the Roman government to do it.

WHY IS SATAN INTERESTED IN HOLINESS?

A sister in the Lord called me to ask me what was going on. She said that she had been praying for me day and night and had to call me. I explained to her that I was trying to get the book *Holy Fire* written, and it has been like a firefight, and I did not know what to do. She said that I had to get that book written, and that was three years ago. I can write a book in five days, and I just finished one in two months because my publisher asked me to do it. So, I decided to trick the devil because I am starting to understand him. Unannounced I went to my studio on my own, and I recorded a fifty-minute CD on Holy Fire. I then finished the artwork and sent it to New York, and it went into production. Right there in New York, everything went haywire. When it was finally delivered to me at my home, it was thrown against my garage door, and all the CDs fell out onto the driveway in the rain. My wife and I just picked them all up and dried them off with hair dryers because we are on to the devil.

The devil does not like that book because it reveals his intent. He knows holiness better than any of us, and he has walked on those fiery sapphire stones in Heaven. His goal is to make sure that you never encounter holiness for yourself. He is trying to keep you out of the type of walk with God that will make you disappear because you have pleased God and He takes you. If Enoch could do it in the Old Testament with no DVDs, no Hillsong, and no Bethel, then you can do it too.

We now have our own TV studios, and eventually we will own everything ourselves to get the Gospel out. This Gospel will go to the ends of the earth—the true simple Gospel of Jesus Christ, and it is free. I am going to give it to everybody and then I am going to go back to Heaven where I was. That is my home; I am just visiting here. I am going to have a cup of tea with Jesus and laugh about how we defeated the enemy.

One day the Lord told me that I would be teaching on holy fire. I waited, and then one day in God's timing I taught on holy fire as a class for my school of ministry. My school was not even in existence at the time, but even so I saw it by faith. I had the best computer that you can get for TV production, but it shut down three times, and finally I said I am just going to preach it. Then we were in New Jersey at King of Kings Church, and I got up to speak on Saturday around the third session. At the forty-minute mark, the Lord told me to stop what I was teaching and start teaching on holiness. I stopped and told everyone that I had to obey the Lord and tell them about holiness. Immediately the whole electrical grid for that half of the city shut down. Even though the building was completely dark, I preached for an additional hour and ten minutes without lights or a microphone. I started to see that if you are being prevented from doing what God has told you to do, you still must stay on the track that He has called you to. I said if George Whitfield can preach to ten thousand people without a microphone, then so can I.

The next day the pastor said that he wanted to take us out, and he drove us about two miles and said, "Here is where George Whitfield preached to those ten thousand." I had no idea. He took us to the place where they stood. It was there that Ben Franklin wrote in his journal that he could hear all the way to the back of the ten thousand people in that town. I had not even known that we were in his area.

Make the devil work for you; make him repay you.

Again, I was preaching on holiness recently, and during worship someone ran in with a large box, left it in the lobby, and ran off. The bomb squad was called in and wanted to evacuate the whole building. I began to realize that there was something that God and satan knew about holiness that we do not know. Why is holiness such a subject of interest? I do not need to understand everything, but I do need to obey God. Even though it is not popular, God told me to drive out the devils by preaching on holiness. Now the box in the lobby turned out to be remarkable. The Lord told a young girl to buy a model jet, which was a replica of the jet that I am believing the Lord for. She did not know that. Not wanting to be a bother, she just left the box in the lobby. That young girl was obedient, and the jet looked exactly like what I was believing my first jet to look like. However, it was not without drama.

It is time to turn the tables on your enemy. What he has done to you has now been found out and not only must he cease in his activities against you, but he must repay sevenfold in recompense. *"But if he's caught, he still has to pay back what he stole sevenfold; his punishment and fine will cost him greatly"* (Prov. 6:31 TPT). You are no longer a victim of satan; you are a child of God. Jesus has defeated him, and now you must tell satan what to do using the name of Jesus!

But the one who indulges in a sinful life is of the devil, because the devil has been sinning from the beginning. The reason the Son of God was revealed was to undo and destroy the works of the devil (1 John 3:8 TPT).

The Lord Jesus bought you back through a conquest with His life and presented mankind back to the Father as His inheritance. Jesus has done an extremely great work for you. This sounds like *everything is rigged in your favor.* This mighty salvation causes you to inherit all the benefits as a son or daughter of God. This is a very important time in your life when all that you have hoped for can come to pass if you will let the Lord bring recompense for what has been stolen from you. You are adopted into the family, and your inheritance is huge.

The apostle Paul wrote to the Galatians concerning their adoption into the family of God.

Yet all of this was so that he would redeem and set free all those held hostage to the written law so that we would receive our freedom and a full legal adoption as his children. And so that we would know for sure that we are his true children, God released the Spirit of Sonship into our hearts—moving us to cry out intimately, "My Father! You're our true Father!" Now we're no longer living like slaves under the law, but we enjoy being God's very own sons and daughters! And because we're his, we can access everything our Father has—for we are heirs of God through Jesus, the Messiah! Before we knew God as our Father and we became his children, we were unwitting servants to the powers that be, which are nothing compared to God. But now that we truly know him and understand how deeply we're loved by him, why would we, even for a moment, consider turning back to those weak and feeble principles of religion, as though we were still subject to them (Galatians 4:5-9 TPT).

God has allowed us to be partakers of His inheritance, but even greater is that in His love for us He gave us precious promises. Through these promises we can be partakers of the divine nature.

By means of these He has bestowed on us His precious and exceedingly great promises, so that through them you may escape [by flight] from the moral decay (rottenness and corruption) that is in the world because of covetousness (lust and greed), and **become sharers (partakers) of the divine nature** (2 Peter 1:4 AMPC).

The enemy must obey you. He must do what you say. Command him to pay you back sevenfold for his activities against you as a child of the Most High God. In the name of Jesus, you are free and more than able to do this and get him working for you. It is about time for him to be in torment instead of you.

In the Fire but Not Consumed!

What we are going through right now is a holy-fire pathway. It will bring you to everything that you have ever desired and believed for in your life. You have to enter into the Holy Fire, and it is not going to hurt you. It is actually going to be fun to have flames and be on fire and not be consumed. Anything that is consumed you do not need. You are released into your destiny right now. You have to stay focused on what God has called you to do because you are special.

Father God said in the Old Testament, *"You've gone into my future to prepare the way, and in kindness you follow behind me to spare me from the harm of my past. With your hand of love upon my life, you impart a blessing to me"* (Ps. 139:5 TPT). This scripture sounds like you are very well taken care of. The Lord has prepared your whole path for your past and your future. Psalm 139:5 is all you need to finish your life out as a Christian. Are you going to be like the religious leaders and be goats, or are you going to be like the lambs that Jesus came back to restore and save? The decision is yours, but I would not wait too long. What is about to happen on this earth will require you to go through that door anyhow, but you do not know it yet.

God has already shown me what will happen in churches everywhere. I have seen churches where they were waiting outside to get in because they heard that if you can get into that service, you will be healed. God showed me that everyone who got into the service was healed. I was standing in line in the future, and I was with people who were talking, and they were not saved. They heard a rumor that if you could get on the last row in the service you could hear God speak to you, actually hear His voice. I say, why wait? You create an atmosphere for Him to inhabit your praises.

> *Then those who feared the Lord spoke to one another, and the Lord listened and heard them; so a book of remembrance was written before Him for those who fear the Lord and who meditate on His name* (Malachi 3:16).

The Lord listened and heard them, and the Lord hears you also. Recording angels wrote the book of remembrance. I have met my recording angel, and you can meet your angel. When you help a widow, an orphan, a child, or someone who cannot pay you back, your recording angel is there. Fearing the Lord and meditating on His name is still for today.

*For thus says the High and Lofty One who inhabits eter-
nity, whose name is Holy: "I dwell in the high and holy
place, with him who has a contrite and humble spirit, to
revive the spirit of the humble, and to revive the heart of
the contrite ones"* (Isaiah 57:15).

God is still holy; He is not old-fashioned but Holy. God is the
High and Lofty One, but He also dwells with the humble and contrite of heart. God revives the spirit of the humble, not the proud.
You can see what our culture has done. So satan has opted you out
of your benefits because he gets you prideful, and then God cannot
dwell with you. The apostle Paul said you have many teachers, but
you do not have many fathers (see 1 Cor. 4:15). I love you, and you
are on my watch, and I am responsible for you, not as your pastor,
but as one who must tell you the truth. God only dwells with the
humble and contrite, and He wants to revive those people. If you are
not revived, that is why He is not dwelling with you. I am not talking
about position; you are still going to Heaven, but I am talking about
relationship. Does He know you, and do you know Him?

God dwells in eternity, but eternity does not dictate who He is.
God is over eternity, and He dwells within eternity, but eternity does
not control Him. God could have forgotten twenty-one days ago to
do something for you. He can come back to twenty-one days ago, do
it for you, and you would never know that He did it. God can do it
without even leaving His throne. When Jesus left me in the operating room, He turned and said, "If you go back for Me, it will count as
extra credit," and then He left. That was twenty-six years ago that He
said that to me. Every time I preach, wherever I go I see Jesus standing there, as well as the operating table. I see the door that is bright
into the glory right in the back of the operating room. I see my body
on the table, and it has not changed in twenty-six years. Every time

I speak under the Spirit, I go to that operating room in the spirit. When I eventually go and be with the Lord, I will find myself behind Jesus through that same door as in the first vision. Jesus will turn and say to me, "Oh, you decided to come with Me." The awesome truth is that the extra time He gave me in order to come back to the earth for "extra credit" was used to influence a whole generation. I decided to outlast the devil.

You can be victorious in this life! Please never, ever forget: *it's all rigged in your favor!*

SALVATION PRAYER

Lord God,

I confess that I am a sinner.

I confess that I need Your Son, Jesus.

Please forgive me in His name.

Lord Jesus, I believe You died for me and that You are alive and listening to me now.

I now turn from my sins and welcome You into my heart. Come and take control of my life.

Make me the kind of person You want me to be.

Now, fill me with Your Holy Spirit who will show me how to live for You. I acknowledge You before men as my Savior and my Lord.

In Jesus' name.

Amen.

If you prayed this prayer, please contact us at info@ kevinzadai.com for more information and material. Go to KevinZadai.com for other exciting ministry materials.

Join our network at Warriornotes.tv

Join our ministry training school at WarriorNotes School of Ministry

More info at
KevinZadai.com

About Kevin Zadai

Kevin Zadai, ThD is dedicated to training Christians to live and operate in two realms at once—the supernatural and the natural. Called to ministry at age ten, he attended Central Bible College in Springfield, Missouri, where he received a bachelor's degree in theology. Later, Kevin received training in missions at Rhema Bible College. At age 31, during a routine surgery, he found himself on the "other side of the veil" with Jesus in a heavenly visitation that forever marked his life. This encounter ushered his ministry into new dimensions of power, activation, and impartation. Kevin is retired after being employed by Southwest Airlines for 29 years; he and his wife, Kathi, reside in New Orleans, Louisiana and are ordained by Dr. Jesse and Dr. Cathy Duplantis.